Practicing Alcohol Moderation

Practicing Alcohol Moderation is designed to be used by clients of behavioral health care providers who have utilized *The Clinician's Guide to Alcohol Moderation.*

This groundbreaking workbook can be used on its own or in conjunction with therapy, and additionally as a resource for family members whose loved ones are struggling with alcohol. It gives transparent, easy-to-follow, research-based explanations with questionnaires, checklists, quizzes, and worksheets. Each chapter begins with a brief overview and is interspersed with exercises and client experiences, combining research-based information with practical self-assessments, tools, and questions to answer to practice alcohol moderation. Readers can take the *Alcohol Moderation Assessment* to determine their likelihood of success in practicing alcohol moderation.

The book provides the resources to create a personalized Alcohol Moderation Plan and suggests ways to manage its success for clinicians and general audiences alike.

Cyndi Turner, LCSW, LSATP, MAC, is the Co-Founder and Clinical Director of Insight Into Action Therapy and Insight Recovery Centers. She is a harm reduction therapist who has been in the addiction treatment field for almost three decades. Cyndi co-developed and facilitates the Dual Diagnosis Recovery Program©, is a clinical supervisor for licensure, expert witness, topic expert contributor for GoodTherapy, therapist for players involved with the NFL Program for Substances of Abuse, and is a nationally recognized trainer on alcohol moderation.

Practicing Alcohol Moderation

A Comprehensive Workbook

CYNDI TURNER, LCSW, LSATP, MAC

Routledge
Taylor & Francis Group

NEW YORK AND LONDON

First published 2020
by Routledge
605 Third Avenue, New York, NY 10017

and by Routledge
2 Park Square, Milton Park, Abingdon, Oxon, OX14 4RN

Routledge is an imprint of the Taylor & Francis Group, an informa business

© 2020 Taylor & Francis

Library of Congress Cataloging-in-Publication Data
A catalog record for this book has been requested

ISBN: 978-0-367-21799-0 (hbk)
ISBN: 978-0-367-21800-3 (pbk)
ISBN: 978-0-429-26617-1 (ebk)

Typeset in Minion
by Apex CoVantage, LLC

Contents

Acknowledgments

I want to express my appreciation to many of the same people as I did in *The Clinician's Guide to Alcohol Moderation: Alternative Methods and Management Techniques* as they were written at the same time.

Book Mommy got even grouchier while meeting the deadline for this one. Kaitlyn and Jacklyn, you are amazing. Both of you helped me stay sane by making me laugh and helping around the house when I needed organization around me. Your independence and drive to do the right thing when no one is looking is beyond each of your years.

Thank you, Mike, for helping me see that we would get through this difficult phase of life. I can't wait to sit on a white sand beach with you.

I appreciate my business partners and friends Craig James and Angie Harris. Craig, without your daily operations we would not impacted the lives of as many people at Insight Into Action Therapy as we did. Angie, without your leadership we could not have opened our intensive outpatient program with Insight Recovery Centers.

Thank you again to the World's Greatest Beta Reader, Bill Schmidt, reader of almost 300 manuscripts, who is also my father. Your copyediting, feedback, and inspirational messages kept me motivated and laughing during this challenging period of my life. Thank you for introducing me to fellow author Russel F. Moran, whose comments helped make my message more understandable.

Chelsea Sievers of Level 27 Media, your images brought my words to life.

I continue to be grateful to all of the harm reduction clinicians who challenged the status quo while I was a young therapist and paved the way for alcohol moderation to become a mainstream treatment option.

Foreword

We are in the midst of a major shift in how we think about drinking and it is essential that we collectively chip away at the dominant abstinence-only mindset that continues to permeate our culture. We owe it to ourselves to have a realistic and sensible conversation about drinking and our relationship to alcohol. Many people who are curious about exploring their alcohol use don't identify themselves as an "alcoholic" and may feel as if there is nowhere for them to seek help or resources about how to consume alcohol in a safer, more moderate way. Thankfully, Cyndi developed this book to help clarify the process and offer useful and practical strategies to help you drink in less harmful ways.

While there is growing support for harm reduction and moderation and our understanding of "recovery" has evolved beyond abstinence as the only acceptable goal, there is still a lot of work to be done. Most programs continue to emphasize abstinence and don't provide options for those seeking non-abstinence goals such as moderation. People are told they have a "permanent disease" and the only remedy is lifelong abstinence. There is no consideration of each person's unique needs, motivation level, and goals—there is only one goal, total abstinence. Those of us who practice harm reduction are still a relatively small community within the United States, and our shared goal is to provide more education and training to both providers and the public about this more holistic and compassionate approach to conceptualizing and addressing problematic substance use.

As Assistant Director of The Center for Optimal Living in New York City and as a former assistant professor at The New School, I've had a front seat to witnessing this paradigm change in our thinking about drinking and drug use. I work closely with Dr. Andrew Tatarsky, a pioneer of harm reduction psychotherapy, and we established The Center for Optimal Living to showcase a more humane and compassionate approach to addressing substance use that extends beyond requiring abstinence. In addition to providing clinical services, we also offer trainings for professionals and the public about harm reduction psychotherapy.

I was honored that Cyndi Turner reached out to me to write this foreword to highlight the important contributions she is making. This book is written in a very clear and inviting style that provides sensible information and tools to help you embark on a journey to clarify the type of relationship you wish to have with alcohol. She also makes good use of vignettes to show the common dilemmas you may face as you work on establishing healthier drinking habits. As Cyndi points out in Chapter 2, the vast majority of people who may be concerned about their drinking do not self-identify as an "alcoholic" and, therefore, don't benefit from a more rigid, abstinence-only approach. We need to expand our thinking about drinking to reduce the shame and stigma in order to help people feel empowered and motivated to make positive changes. This workbook puts you in the driver seat to explore which relationship you ideally wish to have with alcohol and offers practical, tangible tools and techniques to help you attain your goals. Just like changing any other habit, the process begins with an assessment to build increased awareness of your relationship to alcohol.

Cyndi also clearly describes the interaction of biological, psychological, and social factors impacting drinking and how those factors may create challenges as you begin to make changes. By recognizing the ways in which alcohol both helps and hinders your functioning, you can then clarify and map out a new path for yourself which can include controlled drinking, moderation, and/or abstinence. It is also important to pay attention to your motivation level and readiness for change, and Chapter 5 provides a useful overview of these concepts. The Cost-Benefit Analysis will help you gain insight into the reasons for making a change to your drinking patterns along with recognizing the barriers that may interfere with changing your alcohol use. Ambivalence is a natural part of the change process, and helping you gain awareness of the internal conflicts and tension you experience as you begin to change your drinking patterns is really useful. As you acknowledge the positives and negatives associated with drinking, you can then carefully assess and evaluate the role you want alcohol to play in your life.

Cyndi advocates for a period of abstinence in Chapter 6 to help you gain additional insights into your drinking habits, which is also something I encourage my own clients experiment with. Although it may seem off-putting at first to consider taking a break from alcohol, it creates an opportunity to examine how ubiquitous it has become in your life and how it is being utilized as a coping tool, "social lubricant," and companion. Cyndi poses useful questions to help get at what is gained and lost through not drinking. It helps us get better acquainted with how we deal with discomfort and how alcohol may have become the primary tool to provide relief and support. In Chapter 7, Cyndi then describes mindfulness-based strategies designed to bring awareness at the thoughts, emotions, sensations, and circumstances that lead you to crave alcohol in order to establish a plan around how to respond with greater clarity and awareness so that it's more consistent with your goals and intentions. For instance, the SOBER Breathing Space (Bowen, Chawla, Marlatt, 2010) is a mindful check-in process that brings curiosity and compassion to shift how you respond to cravings/urges. Rather than viewing cravings/urges as something to "battle against," by turning towards them with mindfulness, you can begin to understand what is being expressed through the urge and consider new ways of responding. This is a practice I regularly use with my clients (and myself), and we incorporate it in the trainings we offer as well.

The final chapters of this workbook consolidate the information from the previous chapters to help you develop your own "ideal use plan" with alcohol that considers all the assessment data that's been collected throughout. The *Alcohol Moderation Assessment* in Chapter 8 will help you gain awareness of how alcohol has impacted your day-to-day functioning and sets the stage for identifying areas to work on. It is an opportunity to look deeply at your habits and how personal, biological, and social factors are connected to your drinking patterns. Chapters 9 and 10 include realistic and practical information about how to practice moderate drinking that includes examples of strategies you can immediately begin to use. I hope you will find this book a useful guide in helping you improve your drinking habits and create lasting change.

Jenifer Talley, PhD
Assistant Executive Director
The Center for Optimal Living
New York, NY

Introduction

If you picked up this book, it is probably because you or a loved one is struggling with their alcohol use. You may have tried other treatments that were not right for you. They might have required admitting you are an "alcoholic," total abstinence, meeting attendance, relying on a Higher Power, and admitting powerlessness. There is over 50 years of research that shows that you may not have to do any of those to be healthy.

This workbook will help you determine the role alcohol has played in your life and determine if you are ready to make a change to your drinking patterns. You can take the *Alcohol Moderation Assessment*, which will give you predictions on your likelihood of successfully practicing alcohol moderation. Throughout the workbook, I provide you with a rationale for why I give each of my recommendations. I also ask you questions that help you determine what a healthier relationship with alcohol looks like for you. All throughout are tips and tools as well as other people's experiences. By the end, you will be able to write your personalized Alcohol Moderation Plan and have ways to manage its success.

To give you some background about how I got involved in alcohol moderation, I spent the first ten years of my career doing what instinctively worked with the people who sought me out for help with their drinking. It was very different from how most therapists are trained in school. I was using a controversial treatment method called harm reduction, where any change that reduces the consequences of substance use is seen as a success. People were getting better and telling their friends, loved ones, and other professionals about the way I was helping them. Professionals wondered what I was doing differently and clients asked for more assistance outside of their sessions. There were others who could not afford the financial or time commitment that in-person therapy required. I realized that I needed to reach more people. So I spent the next decade researching, writing, and training other clinicians on the harm reduction method called alcohol moderation.

In 2013, I developed the *How Do I Know if I Can Keep Drinking Quiz*. It was originally for clients who were court-ordered to treatment as a result of an alcohol-related legal charge. Once they completed their requirements, they would ask me if they could keep drinking. I knew many of them did not have to completely give up alcohol, so I reviewed the research and developed a tool that could answer this question. My first book, *Can I Keep Drinking? How You Can Decide When Enough Is Enough* came out in 2017. It gave the basics of alcohol moderation. When doing presentations, I met behavioral health care providers throughout the country and learned that, just like me, many had not received any education about harm reduction strategies as part of their training. My goal is to educate all clinicians about alcohol moderation. So I wrote *The Clinician's Guide to Alcohol Moderation: Alternative Methods and Management Techniques*. It is being released at the same time as this workbook and gives a deeper examination of the history, challenges, and methods of moderation with how-to examples.

Those closest to me know that I was dealing with a cancer scare, painful treatments, and severe back issues while I was writing these two books. I really thought I was going to die. But I did not stop writing. This is how important it is to me for clinicians to be trained on harm reduction strategies and for you to have the tools for alcohol moderation. My hope is that both help you have a healthier relationship with alcohol.

Chapter One
Recovery, Harm Reduction, and Alcohol Moderation

What Is Recovery?

How do you define recovery? Well, it depends upon who you ask.

A primary care doctor might say that it is giving the body time to heal after an illness, injury, or surgery. A behavioral health care provider's response will likely have more to do with substance use disorders. They may include something about mental health disorders and their impact on the family. Individuals who just completed an inpatient treatment program are usually taught that recovery is "staying clean." A discharge planner might say that recovery is not using drugs or alcohol and going to Alcoholics Anonymous (AA) meetings. Others may say that recovery is going to an intensive out-patient treatment program or going to a sober living house. Often the response is influenced by the treatment program. Family members' definition may be affected by what they read on the internet. Those who participate in mutual support meetings usually define recovery through abstinence from the substances that rendered them powerless.

What is your definition of recovery?

_____

_____

_____

Did your definition have something to do with having to stop drinking? AA meetings? Having to say that you are an "alcoholic"? Going away to a rehabilitation center?

What if I told you that what you learned about recovery is probably outdated? I wonder if you also felt like you were a failure because you did not believe you were an "alcoholic." Maybe you even attended some AA meetings and felt like you did not fit. You may know you have some issues with alcohol but do not want to totally give it up. You can be in recovery and continue to enjoy alcohol!

In 2011, the Substance Abuse and Mental Health Services Administration (SAMHSA) announced its definition of recovery:

> A process of change through which individuals improve their health and wellness, live self-directed lives, and strive to reach their full potential.[2]

Have you noticed what is missing?

The 2016 Surgeon General's Report on Alcohol, Drugs, and Health says that there are numerous definitions of recovery in relation to substance use disorders. The report states:

> All agree that recovery goes beyond remission of symptoms . . . "abstinence" though often necessary, is not always sufficient to define recovery.[3]

There it is. Abstinence from alcohol or drugs is not necessary to be in recovery! This is such a controversial topic in the field that this concept is rarely taught in schools, presented at conferences, or available as a treatment option. Most people assume that in order to be in recovery you cannot use alcohol or drugs. Did your definition include something about substances?

I cannot stress the significance that experts agree that while abstinence from mood-altering substances is a factor in recovery, it is not sufficient to define this personal process.

Get ready for a change. This workbook is about learning how to have a healthier relationship with alcohol. It may mean changing your drinking habits, but it does not mean that you can never have a glass of wine, cocktail, or beer again. You get to decide. I will teach you how to practice a form of harm reduction called alcohol moderation. It is about you living a healthier, happier life.

What would you like recovery to look like for you?

_____

_____

_____

What Is Harm Reduction?

Edith Springer is attributed with bringing harm reduction to the United States. She was a social worker in a methadone clinic in New York. She traveled to Great Britain during the 1980s and observed how differently they treated their patients.[4] When she returned, she wrote the first article about harm reduction that focused on prevention methods. Springer called it "harm reduction counseling."[5]

Harm reduction takes a preventative approach and respects a person's capacity to change by focusing on their strengths. It focuses on health in relation to substance use rather than morality or legality. The approach establishes safety and educates the substance user. It gives a framework for dealing with substance use and other risky behaviors without requiring abstinence as a goal for treatment or a requirement to receive it.

G. Alan Marlatt called harm reduction "compassionate pragmatism."[6] He believed that it starts with the acceptance that people use substances in ways that negatively affect themselves and those around them. By taking this stance, professionals and alcohol users can collaborate on reducing the risks and effects of alcohol without requiring total abstinence.

Alcohol Moderation Is Harm Reduction

Alcohol moderation is a form of harm reduction. It challenges the way people have been creating public policy and providing treatment in the United States for over 100 years. The tide is turning as you read this chapter. In the early 1990s about 93% of treatment was abstinence-based and required attendance in a 12-step program, traditionally Alcoholics Anonymous. Thankfully, by 2017 that rate dropped to about 77% of treatment programs.[7] While this is an improvement for those who struggle with the requirement of total abstinence, the concept of a Higher Power, and admitting powerlessness, the majority of treatment programs are still faith-based. This workbook requires none of those. You are the one who decides what your recovery is going to look like. This is not a fad or easy way out. It will still take work, but by the end of this book you will have the tools you need. Research shows that reduced drinking approaches are a viable treatment option for the majority of those struggling with their alcohol use.[8]

Client Examples

Below are several examples of how others have successfully utilized alcohol moderation. We focused on their incremental changes and looked at their whole experience, not just their alcohol use. I find that it is better to pay attention to what is working rather than to focus on what went wrong.

Kaitlyn

Kaitlyn, a middle-aged mom, used wine to take the edge off her day. She worked full-time then came home to three kids who had homework to complete, practices to get to, and dinner to eat. She felt that a few glasses of wine would make her a better mom because she thought it made her more patient.

Kaitlyn began to recognize that several glasses of wine a night might be a problem when she almost had a car accident coming home from her daughter's dance class. She'd already had four glasses when she suddenly realized that she'd mixed up her carpool dates, but she still hopped into the car to fulfill her driving duties. She almost had a head-on collision due to her slowed reaction time. She realized that her coping mechanism had put her daughter and two of her daughter's friends' lives at risk, so she called me.

During the initial evaluation, Kaitlyn said that after scheduling the appointment with me, she reduced her intake from an average of five glasses a night to two or three a night. Rather than launching into a discussion about how bad three drinks could be, I said, "That's amazing! How did you go from five glasses a day to two? That's like a 50 percent improvement! What did you do to manage the stress of the kids and dinner and work?"

In this way, Kaitlyn did not continue to beat herself up. She was able to focus on what was working and develop a plan that focused on building upon her successes rather than punishing her for the mistakes of which she was already keenly aware. Kaitlyn wanted to come back to therapy because we developed an individualized plan for her that did not focus only on her drinking, but why she was drinking and what we could do about it.

Jackie

Jackie was a binge drinker on the weekends when her kids went to their dad's house. As soon as her ex and his new bimbo pulled out of the driveway, she began sipping a cocktail while getting ready to go out and hit the meat market. Her ex had already found someone, so why shouldn't she? In therapy we worked together to help her deal with the implications of the divorce on her life. She began to value herself again and figure out what she wanted in a relationship instead of just finding someone to fill the hours.

One Friday night Jackie ran up quite a bar tab. The next night she decided to practice some of the skills she was learning in therapy. She checked out the singles group at her friend's church. She had nothing to drink that night and actually enjoyed herself. In our next session, my response was to give her a huge smile, share in her excitement, and discuss what it was like to have sober conversations where the men were not just looking to hook up.

I focused on the night where she had success rather than on the night where she drank more than she had planned. I helped her identify other situations where she could socialize with other divorcees without alcohol. The next weekend that the kids are with their dad, she is planning to meet up with some other single parents where alcohol will not be present.

Mike

Mike walked into my office with a sad, guilty look. His shoulders were hunched over, and he could barely look me in the eye. Prior to seeing me, he had been going to some AA meetings to deal with his drinking.

Mike hated his job and would often crack the first beer as soon as he got home from work. In the past, he had often polished off a 12-pack by the end of the night. His wife was happy that he had stopped drinking but was frustrated that he was frequently gone in the evenings at an AA meeting. At least when he was drinking, he had been home and could help with the kids a little bit.

Mike was alcohol-free for two months before he couldn't take the stress anymore and went on a bender. He admitted to me what happened and talked about the huge fight that had ensued with his wife. Together, they admitted that they both had issues to work through. They came to the agreement that she would begin working part-time so he could finish his degree and get another job.

Mike expected me to admonish him for drinking, but I was so excited I could barely contain myself. I congratulated him on working as a team with his wife and coming up with a plan together. I looked at what was important—reconnecting with his life partner, with whom he developed a plan for long-term financial stability and happiness for the whole family—rather than focusing on the one night of drinking that resulted from a poor decision. In fact, this decision opened the line of communication that helped this couple regain intimacy and develop a plan to deal with their stressors.

Why Haven't I Heard of Either?

Addiction treatment is a $35 billion industry. Private equity firms, venture capitalists, and all levels of investors view addiction treatment as a lucrative place to put their money. There are two main reasons why the industry is seen as a desirable investment.[9] One is due to the Mental Health Parity Act of 2008 which required insurance companies to offer the same benefits for behavioral health care as they do for physical health care. The other reason is Obamacare, where more people have health insurance.

Both ensure a diversified revenue stream from multiple payors. The goal of many investors is to purchase smaller companies, centralize and automate the process, then sell it as a larger company as a lucrative exit strategy. However, people struggling with their alcohol use are in crisis, not a product that can be made cheaper.

Additional reasons that addiction treatment is seen as a desirable investment sector is because the consumer is dealing with a potentially relapsing condition that may require multiple treatment episodes with several levels of care. The longer someone stays in treatment and the higher the level of care, the more return the investor earns on his or her money. It pays more to label someone an "alcoholic." Investors see long-term use of their services, which equals larger profit.

Lack of Education

For clinicians to practice alcohol moderation, they need to be an experienced, flexible professional. They must be able to practice a variety of treatment modalities and be trained in mental health as well as substance use disorders. It is easy to say that a person must be alcohol- free. That's a clear goal. It is simpler for schools to teach a method that has clear rules and guidelines. I believe that this is why many professionals are taught: If a person drinks, they are an "alcoholic" who needs total abstinence and Alcoholics Anonymous. It is much harder to teach: If a person drinks, it depends on many factors as to what steps you take based on their unique situation.

Challenging a Higher Power

Alcoholics Anonymous has been the primary recommendation for individuals struggling with alcohol use for decades. It is a spiritually based program. To challenge a recommendation that relies on a Higher Power is akin to challenging God. It is hard to challenge the status quo; it is harder when challenging it is akin to heresy.

Call for Change

It is time that we get you the right kind of treatment. For over 50 years, research has shown us that alcohol moderation is an effective treatment option.[10] However, most clinicians and treatment facilities are still practicing with outdated philosophies that have been proven to be unscientific, designed for a limited population, and are not effective for the majority of people struggling with their alcohol use. Public perception regarding those who struggle with their drinking has drastically improved, however, treatment philosophies have yet to catch up. As a result, millions of people are not getting the right kind of treatment and may be unnecessarily suffering.

While it is hard to replace face-to-face meetings with a trained professional, part of harm reduction is sharing information. This workbook will review the process that a clinician might do with you if you were to practice alcohol moderation. It is encouraging to note that several clinical trials found that using a self-help book with self-control tools met their alcohol-related goals as well as those working with counselors using the same tools described in the book.[11,12] You can change your drinking patterns on your own!

If, after completing the exercises in this workbook, you want more help, I suggest looking up Moderation-Friendly Therapists. This is a free service provided by Moderation Management that gives a list of therapists in the United States, Canada, the United Kingdom, Ireland, and Australia that support alcohol moderation.

Read on to learn more about alcohol moderation.

Chapter Two
What Is Alcohol Moderation?

Alcohol Moderation Defined

Before we go any further, let's review what alcohol moderation is. It has been called low-risk drinking, controlled drinking, responsible drinking, and moderate drinking. There are several definitions, all very similar:

The U.S. Department of Health and Human Services and the U.S. Department of Agriculture Dietary Guidelines for Americans 2015–2020 states that moderate drinking is up to one drink a day for women and up to two drinks a day for men.[13] They further stress that individuals should be of legal drinking age, should not be pregnant, should not plan to drive or participate in activities that require skill, coordination, or alertness, should not be suffering from certain medical conditions, and should be able to control the amount they drink.

The American Heart Association's Guidelines recommend an average of no more than two standard drinks per day (28 g/day) for men and no more than one standard drink/day (14 g/day) for women.[14]

The National Institute for Alcohol Abuse and Alcoholism's (NIAAA) definition of low-risk guidelines for alcohol is: no more than three drinks at a time for women/four for men with no more than 14 drinks a week for women and 21 drinks a week for men.[15]

Most countries around the world agree that a low level of alcohol on a healthy adult carries minimal risks. Alcohol in Moderation compiled a worldwide list of Sensible Drinking Guidelines put forth by each country's public health department of their government.[16] In general, they all support the idea that healthy adult men should have no more than two drinks a day; women no more than one in a day, and none if pregnant or breastfeeding. Some countries such as Indonesia and India recommend avoiding alcohol altogether, while Belgium, Malta, and New Zealand recommend some days of abstinence a week and Mexico recommends drinking with food.

DID YOU KNOW? Countries in which people drink regularly tend to have less alcohol-related violence, and fewer accidents, deaths, and suicides. The reason for this is that a binge causes more impairment than regular use. It is worse to have four glasses of wine in one sitting than it is to have the same amount of alcohol over the course of a week.[17]

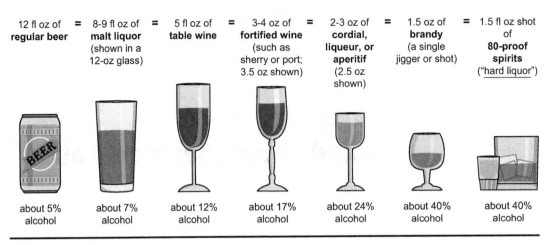

The percent of "pure" alcohol, expressed here as alcohol by volume (alc/vol), varies by beverage.

Image 2.1 Drink Portions

Moderation Management (MM) is a behavioral change program and support group network for people who are concerned about their drinking and want to make positive lifestyle changes. The program is supported by the National Institute for Alcohol Abuse and Alcoholism and is listed on SAMHSA's National Registry of Evidence-based Programs and Practices (NREPP). MM defines a moderate drinker as someone with the following characteristics:

- Considers an occasional drink to be a small, though enjoyable, part of life.
- Has hobbies, interests, and other ways to relax and enjoy life that do not involve alcohol.
- Usually has friends who are moderate drinking or nondrinkers.
- Usually does not drink for longer than an hour or two in any particular occasion.
- Usually does not exceed the 0.055 percent BAC (blood alcohol concentration) drinking limit.
- Usually does not drink faster than one drink per half hour.
- Feels comfortable with his or her use of alcohol, never drinking in secret or spending a lot of time thinking about drinking or planning to drink.[18]

Four to One

In 2019, the United States Census Bureau recorded approximately 329 million people living in the country.[19] Studies show that the majority of individuals (seven of ten adults) drink at low risk levels, with 37% always drinking at low risk and 35% not drinking at all.[20] They point out that about one-third of the population consumes alcohol at levels that put them at risk of alcohol-related consequences. While 28% of the population is drinking at risky levels, only about 6% is drinking to the point that they would meet the criteria laid out in the *Diagnostic and Statistical Manual of Mental Disorders*, 5th edition (DSM-5), for a severe alcohol use disorder (AUD).[21] The other 22% falls into the mild to moderate (AUD) category, for which there are not a lot of treatment options.

To put these numbers in perspective: 6% of the population is about 20 million people—enough people to fill the entire state of Florida. While that is a huge number, the majority of treatment is geared for them. However, there is an even more staggering number: 22%, which represents the number of people who are struggling with their alcohol use. This represents over 70 million people, or about the total number of people who live in the Central Time Zone.

I ask you to do simple math while pondering a question. The majority of treatment programs are geared for those struggling with a severe AUD. Why is most treatment focused on the much smaller number of 20 million, and not the 80 million? This is what is happening in the treatment community. The training, education, funding, and facilities focus on the more severe user, leaving the majority without the right kind of help.

In addition, many people avoid seeking help because they do not want to be labeled as an "alcoholic," attend AA meetings, or accept abstinence as the sole goal of treatment. Giving up drinking is not the only answer for dealing with alcohol-related problems. This workbook will give you tools for alcohol moderation.

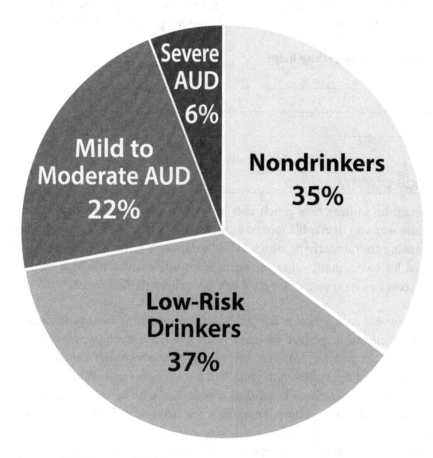

Image 2.2 Types of Drinkers

Why People Avoid Getting Help

Moderation Management (MM) reports that nine out of ten drinkers will not seek help.[22]

That 90 percent of the people who are having problems with alcohol will not seek help is very concerning to me. Many people will continue to suffer because of the mistaken belief that if they are having a problem with drinking, they must be an "alcoholic" and therefore can never drink again. This is even sadder because the drinker is interconnected with many systems: family members, friends, neighbors, and coworkers. One person struggling with alcohol can literally affect hundreds of people, which in turn affects thousands. In theory, this would mean that every person is either directly or indirectly affected by alcohol.

I do not see how applying what works for only a small percentage of drinkers to all drinkers experiencing problems is an effective treatment strategy. We don't treat everyone who has chest pain as if they were having a heart attack. Doctors examine their patients, order tests, and collect more information before they make a diagnosis and provide treatment. Behavioral health care providers need to individualize their recommendations and treatment. Doctors don't perform open-heart surgery on someone who only has heartburn. Similarly, alcohol treatment should be individualized, not given a severe recommendation based on what may be necessary for only the most severe issue.

Additionally, when people get sick from diabetes, cancer, or heart disease, we don't necessarily get mad at them. Instead, loved ones may help them change their diet, research treatments for them, or begin an exercise program with them. We don't get angry and leave them to fend for themselves. We work to help them find different ways to cope. The same should be true for people struggling with alcohol.

What has prevented you from getting help?

_____

_____

_____

The Importance of Why

While it is important to address how much and how often you consume alcohol, it is much more important to explore *why* you drink. If I looked at abstinence as the primary goal and measure of success, I would be missing your underlying issues. While completely refraining from alcohol is a necessary and life-saving goal for some, many other measures for positive outcomes also exist. A different way of determining success can be seen in the way I helped a client named Sarah:

Sarah was a 22-year-old college senior who had been charged with two citations for being drunk in public and was on academic suspension for a low grade point average. Some treatment providers would look at her drinking as the problem. However, upon completing a thorough mental health and substance-use-disorders evaluation, I discovered that Sarah had been sexually assaulted in her freshman year but had never told anyone about it. She was using alcohol to deal with her post-traumatic stress symptoms of insomnia, anxiety, and hypervigilance. Drinking a few beers helped her to fall asleep and not worry about the recurring nightmares of the assault. Taking a few shots before a social gathering helped her forget how anxious she was around the opposite sex, because she now felt all men were predators.

Rather than placing Sarah in the typical mixed-gender substance use education group, I had her participate in several months of individual therapy with me. Our sessions focused on teaching her coping skills to manage the trauma, identifying cognitive distortions, and developing a safety plan. Once these elements were in place, alcohol was no longer a problem for her.

Had Sarah enrolled in a traditional treatment program, she may have been required to attend AA meetings, where she could have become a victim of "thirteenth stepping." This is a practice where some people in AA meetings prey upon vulnerable women and encourage sexual activity as a distraction from alcohol. Additionally, well-intentioned members who mistakenly focused only on her drinking as the problem rather than addressing the trauma she had experienced would have further exacerbated her victim role. This young woman could have walked away with a label that would not have addressed the underlying issues. Instead, through individual therapy she developed other coping skills that dealt with the mental health issues that were causing her to drink.

What are the reasons why you drink?

_____

_____

_____

Do you have any tools or resources to manage them?

_____

_____

_____

Spectrum of Alcohol Use

There is a Spectrum of Alcohol Use. Not everyone who drinks alcohol and experienced a consequence has an alcohol-related diagnosis or even a problem. Most people fall on a continuum of alcohol use throughout their lifespans. An increase in alcohol use is typically gradual. No one becomes an "alcoholic" on his or her first sip.

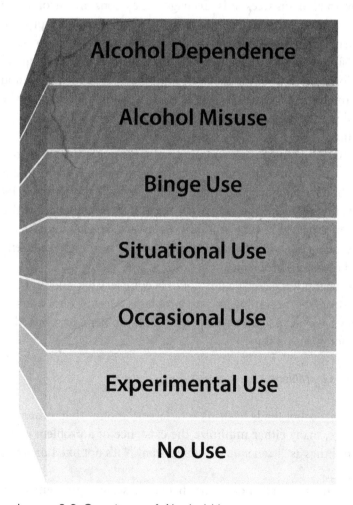

Image 2.3 Spectrum of Alcohol Use

No Alcohol Use: On one end of the spectrum of use are people who do not drink at all. As noted earlier, more than 35% of people do not drink any alcohol. Some people just don't like the effect, feel out of control when drinking, have had a family member with a drinking problem, don't want the calories, or feel it is against their religious beliefs or negatively affects their health.

Experimental Use: This first stage is often due to the curiosity of what alcohol does and what it tastes like. This often occurs during the teenage years. First-time alcohol users often want to see what all the fuss is about. After trying alcohol, some people decide they can take it or leave it. Others will have too much, pray to the "porcelain god," and not drink again for a long period of time, having gained a better understanding of their limits.

A very small percentage of first-time drinkers will describe their first intoxication as "meeting my best friend," "finding the answer to my problems," or "something I couldn't wait to do again." It is like flipping a switch in the brain where it continues to seek the same pleasurable response. This group of drinkers may experience serious consequences if their alcohol use continues. The experimental use of alcohol becomes dangerous when curiosity is quenched, yet the person returns for more.

Occasional Use: Occasional users are not preoccupied with drinking, but they will often drink in social situations. Adults may consume alcohol when they go out to eat, attend a party, celebrate an important event, or want to relax on weekends. Teenagers may consume alcohol as part of an event like homecoming, prom, or a concert. This type of drinking is often not a problem; however, younger drinkers tend to drink more for effect and to binge drink to become intoxicated. This increases the odds for poor decision making and cell adaptation (discussed more in Chapter 8).

Situational Use: Situational use is also not generally a problem. However, the amount and frequency of alcohol use begin to increase. What was once special-occasion drinking now becomes more consistent and associated with specific events such as weekends, parties, birthdays, sporting events, clubs, and other such things.

Binge Use: A binge drinker is someone who consumes a large quantity of alcohol, usually five or more drinks in two hours for men and four or more drinks for women, with the intent of becoming intoxicated. Binging can be a part of normal experimentation as less experienced drinkers do not yet know how alcohol affects them. The person who experiences the consequences of drinking too much and refrains from use for a period of time will most likely not develop a problem. The individual who experiences a consequence yet does the same thing the very next night, weekend, or party may begin to develop an alcohol-related problem.

Alcohol Misuse: This consumption pattern tends not to occur every day and is not a concern every time a person drinks; however, it is beginning to cause problems. Most alcohol users will slow down or stop drinking when they have had a fight, developed a health problem, or received a legal charge. A good way to define alcohol misuse is this:

If it causes a problem, it is a problem.

The person who misuses alcohol tends to drink in a larger amount than others and does so more frequently. At this stage, many either minimize the existence of a problem or deny alcohol's impact. They may say such things as "I can stop anytime I want," "It's not like I drink every day," or "I'm not as bad as _____."

Alcohol Dependence: At this stage, alcohol use has become a serious problem and meets the criteria for a severe AUD. As mentioned previously, only a very small percentage of the population, about 6%, is physically dependent on alcohol. Severe AUD is what many people picture when they think of someone with a drinking problem. This 6% may be who individuals compare to in order to validate that they do not have a drinking problem. This small percentage includes people who drink every day, need alcohol to function, have suffered severe consequences like DUIs (driving under the influence), and have lost something of importance or value to them like a spouse, child, job, house, or health.

This person tends to drink on a regular basis and in large quantities. The individual has developed tolerance, meaning increasing amounts are necessary to achieve the same effect. This person may also experience withdrawal symptoms such as delirium tremens ("the shakes"), seizures, hallucinations, delusions, heart attack, and stroke if denied alcohol. These are dangerous, can be life-threatening, and require medical attention.

People can vacillate on the Spectrum of Alcohol Use over a lifetime. What causes a problem at one time of our lives may not be an issue in another. For example, many individuals in their early 20s drink more than people in their 40s. Does this mean they all have a problem? No. A 22-year-old typically does not have as many responsibilities as a 40-year-old. The younger person can stay out late on the weekend as long as he doesn't make unhealthy decisions when out and gets a ride home if necessary. However, if a 40-year-old stays out until three in the morning, they may neglect their career, spouse, kids, or household chores.

There are many points along the Spectrum of Alcohol Use where you may develop a problem. Sometimes, as your environment changes, your drinking pattern changes. This can be for either good or bad. With conscious effort, you may be able to alter your drinking pattern, amount, and frequency to move to a safer end of the spectrum. That is what this book is about: learning how to practice alcohol moderation.

Where do you fall on the Spectrum of Alcohol Use? Why?

_____

_____

_____

Spectrum of Decreasing Alcohol Use

What follows is a process that occurs when we practice alcohol moderation. There is a lot of information about how alcohol develops into a problem but little on how the problem can be resolved. The Spectrum of Alcohol Use actually has another side: Decreasing Alcohol Use.

With alcohol moderation, you can transition down from heavy use to safer use. This might mean making the decision to change the amount of alcohol use or the situation in which it is consumed. This could include drinking only on weekends, when a parent does not have his or her kids, or not drinking and driving. Safer use can mean decreasing the amount and frequency of alcohol use. While drinking six beers still falls into the heavy alcohol use category, it is better than drinking a 12-pack of beer.

The next step down would be going to controlled use. Again, the amount and frequency might not be at moderation levels, but you are improving. For example, you may drink at a level where you no longer experience a blackout. Or you keep to a limit you decided, even if it is more than 14 a week for women or 21 a week for men. You may reduce your alcohol use it to a level where your blood alcohol concentration (BAC) is lower so that you do not have a hangover the next morning. Or you do not

Image 2.4 Spectrum of Decreasing Alcohol Use

become so intoxicated that you make poor decisions such as engaging in risky sexual behaviors, eating poorly, or damaging loved ones' trust.

The next phase on the spectrum is moderation. This is where you have explored the amount, frequency, intent, and impact of your drinking. The amount falls within moderation guidelines for your gender and generally, you do not drink every day. You are not drinking to the point of intoxication. You have a plan and stick to it.

The other end on the Spectrum of Alcohol Use is abstinence. As is noted in other areas, about one-third of people who attempt alcohol moderation eventually choose to stop drinking. For some, they have determined that they do have a problem with alcohol and decide that complete abstinence is necessary. Others decide that not drinking is preferable to drinking. Some find that it takes too much work to plan ahead and constantly be on guard. One client described it as "petting the dragon." It was too hard for him to have to make a plan each time and it was easier just to make the commitment that alcohol was no longer a part of his life. Another client stated that there was no longer anything she missed about drinking more than she enjoyed being alcohol-free.

Where would you like to fall on the Spectrum of Alcohol Use?

_____

_____

_____

Binge Drinking

Most people who drink excessively are not "alcoholics" who need to quit drinking. In 2014 the Centers for Disease Control and Prevention in collaboration with the Substance Abuse and Mental Health Services Administration found that nine out of ten heavy drinkers are not dependent on alcohol. Even more groundbreaking was that, with the help of a medical professional's brief intervention, most individuals can change unhealthy habits.[23]

Severe alcohol use disorders (AUD) where physical dependence tends to occur is most common among excessive drinkers. About 10% of binge drinkers will have a severe AUD but only 1% of non-binge drinkers will meet criteria for a severe AUD. Binge drinkers do have a higher chance of developing a problem; however, 90% of binge drinkers will not.

Current research repeatedly shows that we need to change how we treat alcohol use disorders.[24] The *Diagnostic and Statistical Manual of Mental Disorders* (DSM-5) was updated in 2013. It recognized that substance use disorders occur on a spectrum from mild, to moderate, to severe. Yet there are not typically therapeutic options that take into account this spectrum. Most treatment remains abstinence-based. My hope is that this book gives you the necessary tools to practice alcohol moderation.

Chapter Three
Self-Assessment

It is more important for you to decide what role alcohol is playing in your life than for me to diagnose you. Most of the time, the only reason I give someone a diagnosis is for billing purposes so the insurance company will reimburse for services. I don't mean to make light of a diagnosis, but it is more important for you assess your relationship with alcohol than for me to give you a code that carries a label that is fraught with stigma.

Diagnosis

The word "alcoholic" is not actually a clinical or diagnostic term. It's a name that people have used since the mid-1800s to describe an alcohol drinker who is experiencing problems. The way that professionals make a clinical diagnosis is with the *Diagnostic and Statistical Manual*, 5th edition (DSM-5). This is the book that clinicians, including doctors, psychiatrists, social workers, therapists, and psychologists, use to diagnose emotional and behavioral problems. As noted at the start of this chapter, insurance companies require a DSM diagnosis to provide reimbursement for behavioral health services.

The DSM-5 came out in May 2013. One of its major changes from the previous edition of the DSM is in the way we diagnose substance-use disorders. Formerly, only two categories for alcohol misuse existed: abuse or dependence. The DSM-5 now looks at alcohol use on a continuum of mild, moderate, and severe.

The information that follows is taken directly from the DSM-5.[25] As you are reading, check off the ones that apply to you:

Alcohol Use Disorder

A. A problematic pattern of alcohol use leading to clinically significant impairment or distress, as manifested by at least two of the following, occurring within a 12-month period:

☐ Alcohol is often taken in larger amounts or over a longer period than was intended.
☐ There is a persistent desire or unsuccessful efforts to cut down or control alcohol use.
☐ A great deal of time is spent in activities necessary to obtain alcohol, use alcohol, or recover from its effects.

- ☐ Craving, or a strong desire or urge to use alcohol.
- ☐ Recurrent alcohol use resulting in a failure to fulfill major role obligations at work, school, or home.
- ☐ Continued alcohol use despite having persistent or recurrent social or interpersonal problems caused or exacerbated by the effect of alcohol.
- ☐ Important social, occupational, or recreational activities are given up or reduced because of alcohol use.
- ☐ Recurrent alcohol use in situations in which it is physically hazardous.
- ☐ Alcohol use is continued despite knowledge of having a persistent or recurrent physical problem that is likely to be exacerbated by alcohol.
- ☐ Tolerance, as defined by either of the following:

  - A need for markedly increased amounts of alcohol to achieve intoxication or desired effect.
  - A markedly diminished effect with continued use of the same amount of alcohol.

- ☐ Withdrawal, as manifested by either of the following:

  - The characteristic withdrawal syndrome for alcohol (see the Alcohol Withdrawal subsection).
  - Alcohol (or a closely related substance, such as a benzodiazepine) is taken to relieve or avoid withdrawal symptoms.

Based on the number of boxes you checked, you can see what degree of an alcohol use disorder (AUD) a clinician might diagnose you:

Mild Alcohol Use Disorder: presence of two to three symptoms
Moderate Alcohol Use Disorder: presence of four to five symptoms
Severe Alcohol Use Disorder: presence of six or more symptoms

DID YOU KNOW? The words *alcoholic* and *alcoholism* were coined in 1848 by a Swedish physician named Magnus Huss. By the end of the 20th century, it had become the accepted way of describing alcohol problems, particularly in the United States where people experiencing problems with drinking were previously called drunkards or inebriates.[26]

Alcohol Withdrawal

Because I believe it is important for you to have accurate information, I have also included the criteria for alcohol withdrawal.[27] Many people are confused about the difference between a hangover—which may include gastric distress, grogginess, nausea, vomiting, and headache—and true alcohol withdrawal. Because experiencing actual alcohol withdrawal can be potentially life-threatening, it is important to determine if you could experience a dangerous medical condition.

A. Cessation of (or reduction in) alcohol use that has been heavy and prolonged.
B. Two (or more) of the following, developing within several hours to a few days after the cessation of (or reduction in) alcohol use as described in criterion A:

1. Autonomic hyperactivity (e.g. sweating or pulse rate greater than 100 bpm).
2. Increased hand tremor.

3. Insomnia.
4. Nausea or vomiting.
5. Transient, visual, tactile, or auditory hallucinations or illusions.
6. Psychomotor agitation.
7. Anxiety.
8. Generalized tonic-clonic seizures (formerly known as gran mal seizures)

C. The signs or symptoms in Criterion B cause clinically significant distress or impairment in social, occupational, or other important areas of functioning.

D. The signs or symptoms are not attributable to another medical condition and are not better explained by another mental disorder, including intoxication or withdrawal from another substance.

Have you experienced any of these symptoms?

_____

_____

_____

Experiencing delirium tremens, or "the shakes," is potentially life-threatening. Alcohol often initially enhances the effect of GABA (gamma-aminobutyric acid), a neurotransmitter that produces feelings of relaxation and calm and can also induce sleep. However, heavy use of alcohol suppresses GABA so that the body requires more and more of it to achieve the same effect, a condition otherwise known as tolerance. Heavy alcohol use also suppresses glutamate, the neurotransmitter that produces excitability. When regular users stop drinking, the chemicals rebound and can cause dangerous consequences such as seizures.

If you have seizures, fever, hallucinations, or delirium tremens, you need to go to the nearest emergency room or call 911 and get into a detoxification program. Potentially life-threatening withdrawal symptoms can begin as early as two hours after the last drink, but the dangerous symptoms often begin to peak around 48 to 72 hours after alcohol cessation. Delirium tremens, however, may not peak until five days after stopping drinking. If you have the shakes, you need to get medical attention immediately, because it can progress to life-threateningly high blood pressure.

Which One Are You?

I begin each of my presentations with an activity. I find that it challenges people's perceptions about who is actually drinking and highlights the concept of the Spectrum of Alcohol Use described in the previous chapter. Based on the percentages that the research tells us, I hand each of the audience members a card. On it may be a picture of a water, donut, cucumber, or pickle. The images each represent a type of drinker.

The first of the four types of drinkers are "waters." They represent 35% of the population. They are the nondrinkers. Many heavy imbibers do not believe that they exist. I often talk about how our normal is what we see. If you spend time with drinkers, you may assume that most people drink. But about a third of the population does not drink at all. Waters generally do not like the taste, want the calories, or like the feeling of intoxication or hangovers. They might have a family member who has a problem, so they abstain. Drinking might be against their religious beliefs, or they would rather eat than drink their calories.

The next group of drinkers encompasses what I call "donuts." Donuts represent 37% of the population. The majority of drinkers fall in this category. Sometimes they order a glass of wine or a cocktail when they go out; sometimes they have water or a soda. Donuts may open a bottle of liquor and forget that it is in their cabinet. They can take it or leave it. If they have too much one night, they will not

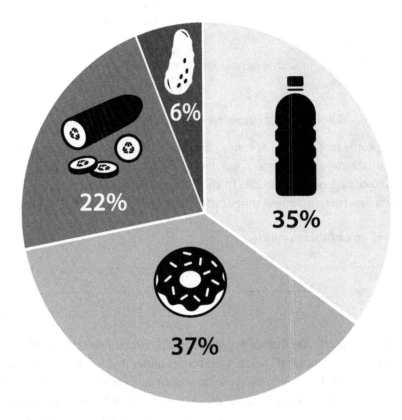

Image 3.1 Which One Are You?

drink again for a long period of time. They rarely drink to the point of intoxication or experience any consequences from their consumption. The idea is: having an occasional donut will not hurt you, but having multiple donuts every day will eventually lead to serious consequences.

> "Having an occasional donut with not hurt you, but having multiple donuts every day will eventually lead to serious consequences."

The third type of alcohol user is what I call "cucumbers." They represent about 22% of the population or about 70 million people. The people in this group are starting to experience problems as a result of their drinking. I say: "If it causes a problem, it is a problem." Cucumbers may have received a legal charge like a Driving Under the Influence or a Drunk in Public. This group may not change their behaviors after their mistakes. They might drink too much one night and do the same thing the very next time. Friends and family are starting to get concerned. Relationships, work, mood, and motivation might be starting to be negatively affected. But, they do not have a physical dependence on alcohol. Clinically, we would say that they are struggling with a mild or moderate alcohol use disorder. Without a change to their drinking patterns, they could move on to the next category: "pickles."

Pickles are cucumbers that have consumed alcohol so much and so frequently that their bodies are likely physically addicted to alcohol. Some say that their insides have become "pickled." As you may hear in an AA meeting: you cannot go back from being a pickle to a cucumber, no matter how bad you want to. However, there are numerous studies that demonstrate that even those in this group benefit from alcohol moderation.[28]

Pickles are often referred to as "alcoholics," or suffering from a severe alcohol use disorder. They represent only about 6% of the population. This group and their loved ones will experience devastating consequences. They will have higher rates of depression and anxiety. Pickles will often get into legal trouble and their actions will negatively impact their jobs, motivation, goals, family, and finances. Pickles experience problems in many areas of their lives. The good news is that the majority of treatments available are geared towards their recovery.

During the activity, I ask each group to raise their hands when I call out the corresponding water, donut, cucumber, or pickle. When a roomful of over a hundred people sees the raised hands of how many people abstain from alcohol use, they are shocked. They are even more surprised to see the percentages of cucumbers who could benefit from a brief intervention like outpatient therapy and education versus the pickles who may truly require abstinence and higher levels of treatment.

Which one are you? Why?

_____

_____

_____

Dominant Drinking Patterns

Another way to self-assess is to examine how you consume alcohol. There are typically four types of drinking patterns:

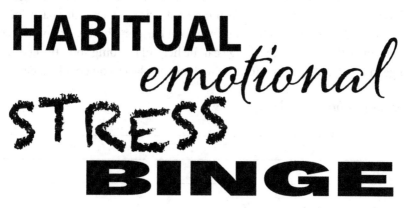

Image 3.2 Dominant Drinking Patterns

Habitual: you drink at the same time, place, or situation. Some examples include: as soon as the game starts, he cracks open a beer; she has a glass of wine while cooking dinner; or the family celebrates events with drinking. By changing the time, place, or situation you may be able to get out of the habit and develop ones that are less damaging.

What drinking habits do you have?

_____

_____

_____

Emotional: you consume alcohol as a way to change your mood. This has also been called self-medicating. You have a drink to loosen up in a social situation. It may be a way to deal with your anxiety, depression, insomnia, or relationship issues. This is one of the reasons it is important to identify why you drink. Once you know your "why," you can identify different coping strategies.

For which emotions do you use alcohol?

_____

_____

_____

Stress: you drink as a way to deal with the fluctuations in your life. You have a fight, then you drink to relax. Problems at work? You hit the bar to unwind. It is important to understand the patterns that you are in and explore ways to either cope with the situation or develop a plan to change the stressful situation.

For what stressors do you drink?

_____

_____

_____

Binge: you have four alcoholic beverages for women/five drinks for men in a period of less than two hours. Your intent is to feel the effects of alcohol. You may not drink on a regular basis, but when you do, it may be hard to stop until the alcohol is gone, everyone has gone home, or you throw up or pass out. Identifying the triggers that lead up to a binge can be helpful in doing something different. It also may require a change in the people you spend time with or the places you go, like a bar, club, or party.

In what situations do you binge drink?

_____

_____

_____

With whom do you drink alcohol to excess?

_____

_____

_____

You may notice that you fit into one or more dominant drinking styles and at different times in your life.

What is your Dominant Drinking Pattern?

_____

_____

_____

Chapter Four
Alcohol's Effect on Body, Mind, and Health

All of us are entitled to unbiased information about what we put into our bodies. I have compiled some of the main effects of alcohol. The impact that drinking has on you individually depends on many factors, including your age, weight, mental or physical health disorders, how much and how often you drink, your gender, the presence of other foods or drugs in your system, and the time period in which the alcohol is consumed. Just Say Know—know the effects of alcohol to make informed choices.

No Safe Level

I know, this may not be a good way to start, but we have new research. A 2016 groundbreaking study that reviewed the impact of alcohol use in 195 countries over a period of 25 years has significant implications.[29] They found that alcohol use is a leading factor in the global disease burden and causes substantial health loss. They reported alcohol use increases the risk of all-cause mortality and is especially true for all cancers. This study was the first one to conclude that there is no safe level of alcohol use.

While there may be no safe level, it does not mean that alcohol is evil or always dangerous. It means that consumption comes with risks. Just as science shows us that sugar and trans fats are not healthy for us does not mean that people do not still enjoy consuming them. Drinking can be a pleasurable experience and accompaniment to many types of celebrations. Recall that I described the majority of drinkers as "donuts." About 37% of the drinking population is consuming alcohol at an amount and frequency that is not causing significant problems. Drinking alcohol is like eating donuts: having one or two occasionally will not hurt you, but having multiple donuts every day is eventually going to lead to serious consequences.

DID YOU KNOW? An occasional glass of red wine may have some health benefits. Red wine contains an ingredient called resveratrol, which may help prevent damage to blood vessels, increase high-density lipoprotein (the good cholesterol), and prevent blood clots. But you can also get resveratrol from grapes and supplements without all of the risks that chronic alcohol use can bring.[30]

Central Nervous System Depressant

Alcohol is a central nervous system depressant. Depressants are a class of drugs that slow down the functioning of your brain by depressing your central nervous system (CNS). The CNS includes the brain and the spinal cord. It controls most of our main functions like taking in information, controlling motor function, thinking, understanding, reasoning, and emoting. The CNS also deals with neurons that form a network that carries information to and from our extremities, muscles, and organs.[31]

Alcohol is one of the most popular depressants. People use it to unwind and relax. The calming effects of depressants can be pleasurable. Initially, one may feel more energized as the alcohol reduces inhibitions and increases socialization. This is why alcohol is often called a "social lubricant." Alcohol can temporarily make people forget their problems. This all sounds like a wonder drug, but what happens to the brain and body when you drink too much or too often?

Brain

The effects of alcohol on the brain are significant. Alcohol interferes with the brain's communication pathways. Drinking alcohol can cause changes in mood and behavior as well as make it difficult to process information and think clearly. It also affects coordination.

The cerebellum, located in the back of the brain, is the area that controls motor coordination. In the short term, damage to the cerebellum includes a loss of balance and resultant stumbling, which increases the risks of accidents and injury. People under the influence also tend to have lapses in judgment and slowed reaction time. These are the main reasons why alcohol impairs your ability to operate a motor vehicle.

The limbic system is responsible for memory and emotions. You may do or say things that are out of character because your inhibitions are lowered, and you may not remember doing or saying them. You may fight when you are intoxicated or become more emotional. You will loosen up with one or two drinks, but an excess of alcohol will alter your feelings and perceptions.

The cerebral cortex regulates your ability to think, plan, and behave intelligently, and it connects to the rest of the nervous system. Damage to it affects your ability to solve problems, remember, and learn. You may identify with these experiences: having the most amazing idea, story, or plan then the next day wondering what was so great only a few hours ago or seeing a video or hearing about what you thought were professional-style dance moves or song lines.

Alcohol affects the neurotransmitters in the brain. These include serotonin, endorphins, and glutamine. You may have heard of serotonin in connection with antidepressants. A certain class of medication prescribed to help with depression is called SSRIs (selective serotonin reuptake inhibitors). Serotonin helps regulate mood. People who suffer from depression are thought to have problems with the levels of serotonin in their brains. Alcohol is believed to interrupt normal transmission of serotonin; thus, people who are regular drinkers may suffer from higher rates of depression than those who do not partake.[32]

Endorphins are another type of neurotransmitter that alcohol interferes with. Endorphins are natural substances that increase feelings of relaxation and euphoria. When you begin drinking, you initially feel good, but over time these important chemicals are damaged. It makes it harder for natural events and experiences to bring genuine happiness and feelings of pleasure.

The third main neurotransmitter that alcohol damages is glutamine. It is believed that glutamine is responsible for memory. Even moderate drinking can cause people to have fuzzy memories. Damage to glutamine production may also contribute to why people who drink heavily black out.

A neuropsychologist with whom I consult describes alcohol as a neurotoxin. Chronic alcohol use causes brain damage. Alcohol alters neurons, which reduces the size of brain cells, shrinking the overall size of your brain. These changes affect a variety of abilities, including motor coordination, sleep, mood, learning, and memory.

Cardiovascular System

Another area that alcohol impacts is the cardiovascular system, which consists of the heart, blood vessels, and blood. Your cardiovascular system is working every second of the day, delivering oxygen and nutrients to your cells and carrying away unnecessary materials.

Your heart is the center of your cardiovascular system. Chronic drinking causes the heart to experience a number of complications.[33] Your heart may develop cardiomyopathy a stretching and drooping of the heart muscle, which weakens your heart and prevents it from pumping enough blood to nourish your organs. Another complication of the heart is atrial fibrillation, an arrhythmia in which the upper and lower chambers of the heart are out of rhythm. This can lead to a blood clot or stroke. Alcohol use also exacerbates the various problems that lead to strokes, hypertension, arrhythmias, and cardiomyopathy.

Additionally, the lifestyle of regular alcohol users can contribute to health problems. Drinkers often have irregular sleeping patterns, smoke cigarettes, use other drugs, and may not eat healthfully or exercise regularly.

Liver and Pancreas

One organ we may not think a lot about is the liver. Your liver's job is to detoxify, synthesize protein, and produce chemicals necessary for digestion. Heavy drinking can cause inflammation, which leads to stenosis (a fatty liver); alcoholic hepatitis (inflammation); fibrosis, a change in the liver caused by inflammation; and cirrhosis, a complication of liver disease which involves loss of liver cells and irreversible scarring of the liver. All of these can be fatal. When your liver is damaged, it can no longer function well and allows toxic substances to travel to the brain. Long-term alcohol use is the most common cause of liver failure.[34]

The pancreas is another organ that does not get a lot of attention until it is too late. Alcohol causes your pancreas to produce toxic substances that can lead to pancreatitis, a dangerous inflammation and swelling of the blood vessels that prevents proper digestion. An attack of pancreatitis is very painful. Research shows that the combination of heavy drinking and cigarette smoking exacerbates the condition.[35]

Immune System

Drinking too much or too often can increase the risk of developing certain cancers, including mouth, esophagus, throat, liver, and breast cancer. Alcohol weakens the immune system, making us more susceptible to diseases and sicknesses. Drinking slows the body's ability to fight off infections for 24 hours after consumption.[36] And think about how often you use the bathroom when you are drinking. How aware of sanitation are you then?

Pregnancy

Alcohol can affect a developing fetus. If a woman consumes alcohol while pregnant, she exposes her baby to Fetal Alcohol Spectrum Disorders (FASD).[37] Symptoms include abnormal facial features and severe reductions in brain function, coordination, emotional control, academic and vocational ability, and socialization. The child's brain will be smaller than normal and have fewer brain cells. They will have lifelong learning and behavioral problems that will likely decrease his or her quality of life.

Driving

Alcohol affects your ability to drive or operate heavy machinery in multiple ways.[38] It impairs your judgment, reaction time, depth perception, coordination, vision, and reflexes. All of these affect your ability to react to the changing situations that occur when driving. The National Highway Traffic Safety Administration reports show that about a third of the people who die in car crashes each year are the result of drunk driving.[39]

Accidents and Injuries

The most common health risk from alcohol consumption comes in the form of accidents and injuries. One study showed that drinking was involved in 38.1% of serious arguments, 56.6% of threats, and 67.9% of incidents of physical aggression.[40] It is significant to note that physical violence was associated with intoxication, not moderate alcohol use.

Sleep

The National Sleep Foundation estimates that 20% of Americans use alcohol to help them fall asleep.[41] While it may increase drowsiness, the reality is that it actually worsens the quality of sleep. It decreases the time spent in the most restful and restorative stage: REM. This is where we experience rapid eye movement and is where we dream. Dreaming is necessary to store and encode memories.

Drinking alcohol before bed is linked with more slow-wave sleep patterns known as delta activity. This is where we experience deep sleep that allows for memory formation and learning. However, alcohol turns on alpha activity, which should occur when we are sitting quietly, not during the night.

While you may fall asleep quickly after drinking, it is also common to wake up in the middle of the night. Alcohol affects the normal production of chemicals in the body that trigger sleepiness and subside once enough sleep has occurred. After drinking, production of adenosine (a sleep-inducing chemical in the brain) is increased, allowing for a fast onset of sleep. But it subsides as quickly as it came, making you more likely to wake up before adequate rest has occurred. Drinking alcohol also impacts your ability to stay asleep as it is a diuretic, requiring trips to the bathroom.

Alcohol also interrupts our circadian rhythms. These rhythms help our bodies stay in sync with a 24-hour day like an internal clock that sends signals for things like digestion, hormones, and temperature regulation. Additionally, alcohol relaxes the entire body. This sounds great, but it also relaxes the muscles in our throats. This makes you more prone to snoring and potentially life-threatening sleep apnea.

The National Health Service in the United Kingdom notes numerous ways that a lack of sleep can impact us.[42] Missing just an hour and a half decreases our alertness, putting us at risk of accidents and injuries. It impairs our ability to think and transfer information that we saw, heard, and learned throughout the day into our long-term memory so that we can recall it in the future. Lack of sleep impairs our mood, which can affect our relationships with the people around us.

This also makes us less likely to participate in healthy activities like eating well, socializing, or exercising.

Chronic sleep deprivation adds up and becomes more serious. These impacts include high blood pressure, heart attack, stroke, obesity, and decreased sex drive. Long-term lack of sleep also affects our appearance. Over time it leads to premature wrinkles and undereye circles. Research also shows that impaired sleep increases cortisol, a stress hormone. Cortisol is known to break down collagen, the protein that keeps our skin looking young and smooth.[43]

Weight

While alcohol is fat-free, it is terrible for weight management.[44] Most alcohol has double the amount of sugar as most carbohydrates. It is also calorie dense, with almost twice as many calories as in protein or carbohydrates. Alcohol also slows the body's ability to burn fat. Once it gets into your body, it gets converted into acetaldehyde, then acetate, and finally acetyl-CoA. These are inefficient fuel sources. The body cannot store these metabolites. Your body has to burn these off first and other fuel sources like fat and sugar must wait. Ultimately, alcohol puts your body in a fat-storing mode. Whatever you are eating while drinking will be stored while the effects of the alcohol are being processed.

Not only does alcohol lower inhibitions, making us more susceptible to making poor food choices, but it also activates an area of the brain that regulates food intake.[45] Nerve cells make a protein called agouti-related proteins. These stimulate food intake. So we are getting a triple whammy of impulsive eating, lowered metabolism, and increased appetite.[46]

Risk Analysis

The information listed in the previous section can be overwhelming. It is not meant as a scare tactic, but information about how your drinking could affect you. It may sound as if all alcohol consumption is bad. Heavy, chronic, and binge drinking are typically associated with the worst consequences. While alcohol cannot be considered "safe," most drinking is pleasurable and without problems. You have to determine what role alcohol has played in your life and decide what you would like it to be in the future.

Which of the above areas concern you?

_____

_____

_____

What were the results of your last physical? (Hint: you need to go get one!)

_____

_____

_____

Do the benefits of your current alcohol use outweigh the risks?

_____

_____

_____

What could you change to bring your drinking to a safer level?

_____

_____

_____

Chapter Five
Am I Ready to Make Changes?

At this point, you should have a sense of where you fit on the Spectrum of Alcohol Use, what your DSM diagnosis might be, and what your Dominant Drinking Pattern is. You may have decided that you do not like your current relationship with alcohol. Before we jump into trying to make changes, which you may have already attempted and not liked the results, I suggest we look at your readiness to make a change. This is important because you may be getting pressure from others to do something different, but you are not yet ready. All are going to be frustrated until we have a plan of action.

Stages of Change

The following Stages of Change model can be helpful when determining your readiness to make changes to your drinking patterns. James Prochaska and Carlo DiClemente developed the Stages of Change Model in the late 1970s.[47] They were studying how smokers were able to give up the habit, but it applies just as well to alcohol use. They noted that change occurs through an individualized process of stages.[48]

Precontemplation

If you are in the Precontemplation Stage, you may not consider your alcohol use a problem. You may not yet have experienced any negative consequences, or you may not be ready to acknowledge the severity of consequences that have already occurred. You are not ready to acknowledge that there is a problem behavior that needs to change. At this stage, loved ones may be expressing concern, but you are not ready to hear it. It may be helpful to talk with them about the impact of your drinking on them. Sometimes this can help if you tend to minimize how bad it is. Often consequences occur before you are ready to move to the next stage.

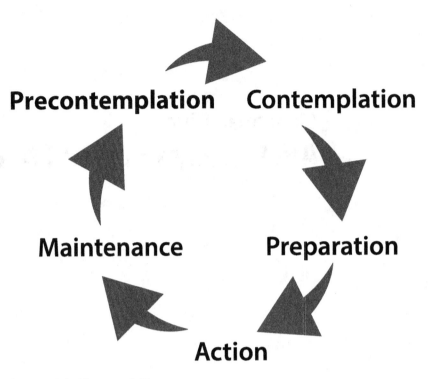

Image 5.1 Stages of Change

Contemplation

If you are in the Contemplation Stage, you are beginning to acknowledge a problem with your drinking and may be thinking about taking steps to make a change. You might have tried to cut down or modify drinking patterns, but you are not yet ready to make substantial changes. A good example of the Contemplation Stage occurred with Lauren:

> *Lauren was a 30-year-old single professional. As part of her job, she attended quite a few marketing events, which were often held in bars or restaurants. Initially, Lauren was very nervous with the social aspect of her job and uncomfortable with the idea of trying to sell herself to get new business. When she first started, she would have a glass of wine or two to help her loosen up and feel more comfortable. Recently she noticed that her two glasses of wine had turned into three or more, and she went home with some of her male colleagues on more occasions than she would like to admit.*
>
> *After a binge, Lauren would feel so embarrassed and guilty that she would go to the store for a bottle of wine to drink away her feelings regarding the night before. She was late to work a few times because of a hangover and avoided certain work functions for fear that she would run into one of her one-night stands.*
>
> *Lauren wanted to get married and began to wonder whether the guys she kept picking up were marriage material. A few of her friends expressed concern about how much she was drinking and the choices she was making. She wondered if perhaps it was time to talk to a therapist. But she would always get too busy and decide to wait until after the holidays or some other event.*

Lauren was ambivalent about making changes. She was on the fence, not ready to do something anytime soon. A good friend or therapist could validate that Lauren is not sure whether she should make some lifestyle changes and let her know that any decisions she makes would be hers. Someone could help her weigh the pros and cons of any changes and come up with a plan on how to deal with each. I would have her consider an answer to these questions: "If you were to make a change to your drinking, what would it look like?" and "What are you most concerned about if you decide to change how you drink?"

Giving Lauren unbiased education and information could also be helpful in assisting her to make a decision. If people are too harsh and confrontational, she may revert to denial, or she may feel bad and continue her drinking patterns secretly to deal with those negative feelings.

You move out of the stage of contemplation when making a conscious decision to change your alcohol behaviors.

Preparation

When you are in the Preparation Stage, you are ready to alter your drinking patterns. You have likely begun planning how to make the changes and are prepared to take action. It can be overwhelming to decide where to start and what should be done. This is why is helpful to obtain additional resources and identify a support system. We will review all of these in the next few chapters.

Action

In the Action stage, you are making changes to your drinking patterns. Meeting with a therapist can be helpful. That person can give you support and accountability, explore with you how well the changes are working, and forecast potential problems while developing solutions with you. I often ask things like: "How is that working for you? Your family?" "Is that something you think you can keep doing?" and "What is coming up that might get in the way?"

Over a lifetime, you may cycle through many of these stages. The coping skills that worked in the past may cease to help as new life challenges arise. You may have the best intentions yet still struggle with maintaining changes with your drinking patterns.

Maintenance

The Maintenance Stage occurs after you have changed your drinking patterns. The goal now is to keep the healthy behavior going to prevent a relapse to the old behavior. Many of my most successful clients schedule regular check-in appointments with me. They have worked long and hard to get to where they are in their recovery process and do not want to go back to where they were. Some of them have chosen complete abstinence, and some are working on drinking in moderation.

An example of successful maintenance occurred with Joe:

Joe was a 65-year-old who had just retired from a long career in the military and then the private sector. He was married and had three kids who had finished college and moved out to begin their own lives. He and his wife were finally living "the life." They had retired to a warm climate, and Joe spent his days golfing and nights playing cards or shooting the breeze with friends.

Joe was a Scotch drinker. Throughout his life, he'd had periods where his drinking was too much. In his 30s, he had attended an intensive outpatient program and some AA meetings. In the last few years, he had been seeing a therapist who was helping him develop an Alcohol Moderation Plan. The plan included drinking only one night of the week, not before 5 p.m., and never consuming more than three drinks at a time.

Joe had begun noticing that he was having a few beers on the golf course and that his neighbor was providing bourbon during their weekly poker games. He realized that both the amount and frequency of his drinking were creeping up again, and his wife was complaining that he was becoming moody and irritable. He made an appointment with his therapist and began reworking the moderation plan.

Joe's alcohol use and consequences varied over the years. His drinking was not as bad as it had been at other times in his life, but he did not like the person he was becoming as his recent drinking increased. He and his wife had saved for a lifetime to be able to travel in their later years. If his alcohol intake continued to escalate, he worried that his health would begin to suffer, and he would not be able to enjoy his grandkids or take that European vacation.

Joe made the decision to check in with his therapist to rework his plan. He decided on a period of complete abstinence again. Once his system had been clean for a few months, he was able to have his weekly Scotch but eliminated beer on the golf course and the liquor during poker night. Both games improved as a result.

People often move through the stages described above sequentially. However, Prochaska and DiClemente realized that people may skip a stage or move forward and backward through them. I have found that people cycle through the stages over a lifetime. We may resolve an issue, but then a crisis or a life change happens and we need to readjust to the stages.

What stage are you in now? Why?

_____

_____

_____

What would it take to move you to the next stage?

_____

_____

_____

What concerns do you have about making changes?

_____

_____

_____

DID YOU KNOW? The idea that it takes three weeks to form a habit is attributed to Dr. Maxwell Martz, a cosmetic surgeon. He reported in his book that it took patients an average of 21 days to get used to a new image after surgery. Over the years, this was misquoted so many times that people began to believe this was actually data from a study.[49]

Cost-Benefit Analysis

Another step that can be helpful before making a change to your drinking patterns is to do a Cost-Benefit Analysis. I do this in a way that is different from most. Usually, the goal is to determine that there are more consequences to drinking so that you will decide to make a change. I actually want you to identify the benefits so that you can make a plan to deal with the good things that drinking was doing for you. Too often alcohol is seen as all bad. By ignoring the benefits, a person's change plan is doomed to fail.

Most loved ones, health care providers, and legal professionals focus on quadrants 2 and 3, the consequences of drinking and the benefits of not drinking. Traditional treatment programs still spend much of their focus on the impact of alcohol use. The information is provided in a "scared straight" manner. However, studies have shown that this type of education does not yield an effective long-term impact.[50]

Quadrant 2 explores the cons of drinking, while Quadrant 3 looks at the pros of not drinking. Almost everyone has some idea of the negative impacts of their alcohol use. I'm sure you can list numerous legal, health, relational, and mood problems. I do encourage you to fill out the whole exercise. It is one thing to think about all of the consequences over a period of time; it's quite another to see it all listed in one place.

While it is important to acknowledge all of these areas, I find it is much more helpful to look at the pros of drinking and the cons of stopping.

I have found that the most effective change occurs when we explore the first and fourth quadrants: the pros of alcohol use and the cons of not drinking. It is crucial to identify and acknowledge the

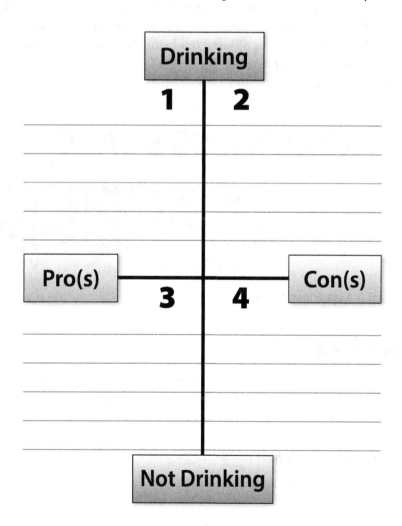

Image 5.2 Cost-Benefit Analysis

benefits of your alcohol use. Obviously, you would not have continued to drink if it were all bad. The severe consequences often do not begin until years into the established drinking patterns. Exploring the benefits of drinking accomplishes several things. You may not have realized *why* you were drinking. Once you do, you can identify additional tools to manage those areas. You also may be able to find a way to reduce the consequences and maximize the pleasures of alcohol use.

When you identify the cons of not drinking, you can better develop a plan for changing your drinking pattern. You may find that it is only necessary to change the situations in which you drink or the amount and not actually have to completely give up alcohol.

What do you notice after completing your Cost/Benefit Analysis?

_____

_____

_____

Readiness Scale

Now that you have completed your self-assessment, determined where you fit in the Stages of Change, and performed a Cost-Benefit Analysis, it's time to look at your readiness to take the first step. On a scale of one to ten, with one being "not at all" and ten being, "let's start now," how ready are you to make a change to your drinking patterns?

Check where you feel you are on the Readiness Scale.

Image 5.3 Readiness Scale

Why did you choose that number?

_____

_____

_____

What would it take to get you to the next number?

_____

_____

_____

Importance Scale

The next scale assesses how important it is to you to make a change to your drinking patterns. On a scale of one to ten, with one being "not important at all" to ten being "the most important thing to me now," how important is it for you to change your drinking patterns? Check where you feel you are:

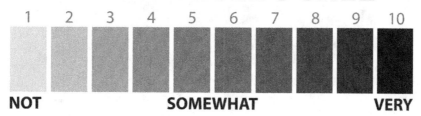

Image 5.4 Importance Scale

Why did you choose that number?

_____

_____

_____

What would it take to get you to the next number?

_____

_____

_____

Once you have the answers to these questions, you are ready to move on to the next chapter: "Why Four Months." You may not be happy with what I am about to suggest, but I give you the rationale for why I do!

Chapter Six
Why Four Months

This chapter may seem out of place with my message about alcohol moderation. I recommend that before you try to moderate your drinking, you actually stop drinking for a period of time. I have found that my clients achieve the best results when they remain totally abstinent from alcohol for four months. Other research has found that individuals who go through a period of abstinence are more likely to reach their alcohol-related goals.[51] This chapter will explain the rationale and review tools for obtaining alcohol-free time.

Rationale for Four Months of Abstinence

Some moderation programs recommend being alcohol-free for 30 days. I find this is often not long enough. Most of us can make a change for a short period of time but struggle to maintain it long-term. Of the many New Year's resolutions you have made, how many have actually become part of your day-to-day life? I am a regular gym user. In my gym, the classes fill up during the month of January and I often must wait to use the elliptical, or I have to search for the weights I want to use for a particular workout. However, by March I have my pick of all the equipment. That's because most people's good intentions fizzle out after a few weeks.

Many of us struggle to make lasting change. You may be familiar with the term *white knuckling*. Some say it originated with nervous flyers who gripped the armrests of their seats so tightly that their knuckles turned white. I believe many drinkers trying to change their patterns metaphorically do this. They hold on for a while and muscle through some alcohol-free time. Sometimes this is to prove to themselves or someone else that they don't really have a problem and can stop at any time. The concern is that during this time they may not be dealing with the internal reasons for their drinking and therefore are not developing necessary coping skills.

I actually want you to feel some discomfort during this period of abstinence. This gives you the opportunity to identify why you have been turning to alcohol. Once you know this, then you can develop a reasonable plan of action.

Some people try to justify their drinking by saying they drink out of habit, not because of negative emotions like sadness or anger or to avoid something painful or uncomfortable. Even so, I still recommend four months of not drinking. This will enable you to go through an entire season of events without alcohol. If you go four months without drinking, you will likely have to come up with a plan for handling holidays, birthdays, anniversaries, parties, sporting events, annual get-togethers, and other such events without relying on alcohol.

> *Ed was an intelligent, independent 39-year-old IT guy who was responsible for a large government department. The stress and long hours were killing him. He discovered that one or two beers helped him relax and fall asleep, but these soon turned into four or five beers and sometimes some bourbon as well. Ed was a runner and did not like the gut he was developing from his excessive drinking.*
>
> *Ed came to me looking for help for his insomnia and stress. When I suggested that he might want to be alcohol-free before we addressed those issues, he looked at me in horror, saying, "But how will I function? I can't sleep without it." I assured him that I wasn't asking him to start that night. My job was to give him some tools to manage life better. I don't take away a client's primary coping skill of drinking (unless they need to be medically detoxed) before helping them to develop new ones. As Ed implemented new coping skills, he found he could fall asleep faster and actually had a better quality of sleep without alcohol.*

People often fight me about going through this period of abstinence. They argue that they are not "alcoholics." I agree. But you picked up this book because alcohol was causing some type of problem in your life.

You know what it feels like to be a regular drinker, but you may not remember what life is like without alcohol. You need to address your concerns related to not drinking, plan for risky situations, and develop alternative ways to relax, socialize, cope, etc. I am not suggesting never drinking again, only a period of four months. You may be surprised at the new perspectives you gain about yourself and the people around you.

One of the main reasons I recommend four months of alcohol-free time is for you to see how you handle a wide variety of situations without alcohol. During this time, you may experience some discomfort. The goal is to learn other coping skills besides using alcohol. Being chemically free also helps bring emotions to the surface, thus giving you an opportunity to manage life in a different way.

Some people initiate therapy at this point. You also may find help with online programs like Moderation Management, HAMS (Harm reduction, Abstinence, and Moderation Support), or Hello Sunday Morning. It can also be helpful to let those closest to you know that you are going through this process so they can offer support and accountability.

When thinking about an alcohol-free period of time, you may focus only on negative emotions such as anxiety, stress, depression, boredom, and anger. I want to remind you that while alcohol numbed these negative emotions for you, drinking also dulled positive feelings like joy, awe, love, compassion, and empathy. The range of emotions that you will experience when you are alcohol-free may pleasantly surprise you. You may also enjoy feeling more stable. When drinking, life can feel like sharp, jagged ups and downs. My clients report that abstinence feels more like manageable, rolling waves.

This period of abstinence should also give you enough time to break any unhealthy patterns. Then you can determine to what degree you want alcohol to be part of your life after the four months. The distance allows you to see patterns. By stepping away, you can get a different perspective.

I have found that about half of my clients who go through a period of sobriety actually chose complete abstinence even when this was not their goal at the outset of treatment. Once people experience some alcohol-free time, they often find that it is better than what they imagined, as they were only focused on what they would lose, not what they could gain. Drinking or not drinking becomes less of a focus when you shift your attention, time, and activities to other opportunities. I recommend that you say "I choose not to drink" rather than "I can't drink." The former implies empowerment rather than deprivation.

Many people's first response to hearing when I recommend being alcohol-free for four months is like Sal's:

Sal, a self-employed mechanic in his 40s, stared at me in shock. I had just recommended that he try four months of abstinence. He thought he was in the wrong place. He asked if I was the lady that did not believe that all drinkers were "alcoholics" and wouldn't make him go to those meetings for quitters.

People in his life were telling him that he had to admit that he was an "alcoholic" and say he was powerless. I let him know that my goal was to empower him. The way to do this was to gain clarity by feeling the discomfort that he had been trying to drink away and see what new feelings emerged. He didn't jump up and leave the room, so I let him know that during the four months of abstinence we would observe, together, what he was experiencing and that I would help him develop coping skills as well as identify how and when positive ones surfaced so that he could repeat those.

I let him know that I would be his biggest cheerleader when he experienced success and would teach him how to build upon the wins. I also told him that I would challenge him if he continued to make poor decisions. In this way, I offered him not only support and encouragement but also the necessary accountability for when he felt hopeless or his willpower wavered.

What was your reaction to reading that I suggest four months of being alcohol-free?

_____

_____

_____

What are you concerned about happening if you give up drinking for a period of time?

_____

_____

_____

The areas that you just listed above should be your starting point. You don't need to start the period of abstinence right away. However, sooner is better. There will always be an event or reason for you to procrastinate. I have always said that Nike has the best slogan: Just Do It.

Just do it does not have to mean giving alcohol up right away. It means coming up with a plan of action for *how* to do it. Identify the events and emotions that concern you and use your support system to help you get through them.

This section discusses some helpful skills to successfully abstain from alcohol for four months. Alcoholics Anonymous (AA) has a great acronym for sober:

Son
Of a
Bitch
Everything is
Real

This is exactly I want to happen for you. Deal with life on life's terms. Regular alcohol use takes the edge off so that life feels out of focus. Abstinence allows you to gain clarity to see reality and identify changes you want to make. Maybe your relationships are stressed because of your drinking. During the alcohol-free time, you can learn better communication skills that will lead to greater intimacy. I point out to my clients that when they stop drinking, they have a more even playing field in their relationships. Trust can be regained, and they have more of a voice when they take drinking as an issue off the table.

Additionally, without the salve of drinking, you may realize that it has been affecting your motivation to make beneficial lifestyle changes. Many of my clients are frustrated with themselves when they realize that their alcohol use was covering up a problem rather than helping them cope. Without alcohol, they have their full faculties to make changes. Most are happier with less alcohol because they can more fully enjoy, rather than tolerate, their lives.

In the early days of abstinence, you may feel emotionally raw. Some of this is from the effects of alcohol on your brain and body. It will pass. I tell you this because many people mistakenly believe that that is what sobriety feels like. You can get through the detoxification process sooner by drinking water, eating a balanced diet, and exercising.

Alcohol may be your primary way to relax, socialize, and have fun. What did you used to enjoy prior to your regular alcohol use? Keep in mind that nothing that is healthy in the long run will work as quickly as alcohol did, but know that other activities will likely not have the same physical, emotional, relational, and financial consequences that regular alcohol use had on you.

Boredom is one of the main causes of relapse.[52] We all need something to look forward to each day, whether it is enjoying a good cup of coffee, working out, chatting with a coworker, snuggling with our mate, or watching our favorite show or sporting event. On a weekly basis, we need something that gets us excited. Maybe it's having dinner with friends, going to a movie, participating in a community event, or seeing a show. We also should have bigger things to look forward to, like planning a getaway, crossing something off our bucket list, or taking a road trip.

DID YOU KNOW? Alcohol is terrible for insomnia. Some think that a few drinks before bed helps them fall asleep faster. But once they fall asleep, their quality of sleep is poor. Alcohol reduces REM (rapid eye movement), the restorative stage of sleep where dreams occur. This disruption causes daytime drowsiness and poor concentration. Alcohol can also suppress breathing, thus increasing sleep apnea and snoring. Rest is also disturbed as alcohol is a diuretic that requires trips to the bathroom.[53]

One of my best friends has a great idea to help him experience life. He gets his local recreation guide and picks a number from one to whatever the number of pages in that quarter's issue. Then he opens the guide and picks an activity from that page. As a result, he has done some interesting activities, met some fun people, and has funny stories from the activities that were flops. The idea is to get out and do something. You may not like nine out of ten things you try, but the tenth one may become a new hobby or passion, and you may make some great friends along the way. Your homework from me tonight is to do something fun.

Gain/Lose

Before we move on to the next chapter, I want you to do two exercises. I want you to identify what you think you will lose by giving up drinking for a period of time. Your first instinct will be to think of all the good things you will miss out on like events, and what it did for you. I also need you to contemplate what you may gain by taking a break from alcohol. You may lose a few pounds, sleep better, spend less money, wake up earlier, do other activities, be on better terms with your family, or have more sex because you are not affected by alcohol and your mate is not angry with you. I promise there will be more pleasant surprises than you can imagine.

What will you lose during the alcohol-free period of time?

_____

_____

_____

What could I gain during the period of abstinence?

_____

_____

_____

Breakup Letter

The second exercise is to break up with alcohol—well really, tell it you are going on a break. We will let Ross and Rachel from *Friends* decide which it is!

If alcohol were a person, what would you say to them as you are entering this period of abstinence? You may review some of the negative reasons you are taking a break. You may also tell alcohol why you are choosing to go without it for a while. Be open and let it flow. This is for you. No one is going to read this. Don't be surprised if you get emotional. Alcohol may have been a major part of your life since you were a teenager and your companion at social events for decades.

Dear Alcohol,

_____

_____

_____

_____

_____

_____

The next chapter will go over tools to help you get through the four months. It won't be as bad as you think!

Chapter Seven
How to Achieve Four Months of Abstinence

I am glad you kept reading. That means you are ready to explore what it takes to be alcohol-free for a period of time. Throughout this chapter, I will review some strategies that will help you get through this process successfully.

Mindfulness-Based Relapse Prevention

In the last chapter, I used an acronym to describe sober and what I hoped for you during the four months of going without drinking. This is another way to get SOBER. I like the play on words because people tend to remember acronyms better. What follows is a mindfulness-based relapse-prevention technique that breaks down the word *sober* and recommends steps for each of the letters:[54]

Stop
Observe
Breathe
Expand
Respond

S—STOP: get out of autopilot mode. By this, I mean stop doing things automatically without being fully aware of what you are doing. For example, think about how you can get into your car to run errands, then a few minutes later you somehow end up at the first store on your list. You did not consciously tell yourself to turn here, speed up, stop, go left, or park. Your brain just ran with the thought and got you there. This works well for mundane situations, but think of the times when you run on autopilot regarding unhealthy behavior. You get in the car and automatically light up a cigarette. Maybe you sit on the couch, turn on the television, and unconsciously finish a whole bag of chips. Many people do this with their drinking, too.

The danger of running on autopilot occurred with Michelle:

Michelle's goal was to remain abstinent from alcohol. She did not like the consequences that her drinking caused to her health and her family. She had made it nine months without a drink. Then she attended a large family gathering in a restaurant. The table was set beautifully to include both water glasses and wine glasses. The server promptly filled both for all adult guests.

Michelle was happily chatting with her favorite cousins. She was so involved in the conversation that she did not notice that she drank an entire glass of white wine, which the waiter dutifully refilled. It was not until she got up to use the ladies' room that she realized she was a little tipsy. She was angry with herself, and her husband stared at her accusingly later that night.

Michelle was drinking on autopilot. Though she had no intention to consume alcohol at this event, she had also made no active effort not to drink. If she had been more mindful, she may have been more successful in maintaining her sobriety. She could have had a conversation with her husband beforehand, asking for his support; asked the waiter to remove her wine glass; or ordered her favorite nonalcoholic beverage before she got swept up in the emotion of the event.

In what drinking situations do you run on autopilot?

_____

_____

_____

O—OBSERVE: observe your emotions, urges, physical sensations, and thoughts. In other words, know your triggers. Many drinkers spend a lot of time thinking about drinking, being under the influence, or recovering from the impact of drinking. As you enter early abstinence, I want you to know that you may experience a heightened sensitivity to your environment. It is called Post Acute Withdrawal Syndrome or PAWS. Don't worry; this is not a permanent state. I share this because this is why many people give up abstinence in the early days. They think, "If this is what being alcohol-free feels like, I don't want it."

Be aware of how you feel as you go into a drinking situation. You may notice certain reactions in your body before they actually become conscious thoughts. These may be signals that require your attention and action. The more aware you are of what is going on internally, the better you can deal with your external enjoinment. Understand that giving in to a momentary urge may not yield the best outcome for you in the long term.

Think back to a recent craving you experienced:

How did your body feel physically?

_____

_____

_____

What did you feel emotionally?

_____

_____

_____

What did you want to do?

_____

_____

_____

What did you do?

_____

_____

_____

What can you do differently next time?

_____

_____

_____

B—BREATHE: pay attention to your breathing. Are you breathing in and out slowly and evenly? Are both your chest and your stomach rising and falling with each intake and exhale, or do you sometimes gulp for air? Do you sometimes hold your breath? Is your breathing rapid and shallow? Focus on your respiration; it can tell you a lot about how you are feeling.

Breathing is something we do unconsciously thousands of times a day. A change in normal breathing can signify that we are experiencing negative emotions. When we get upset, angry, scared, or nervous, we tend to go into fight-or-flight mode. In this reaction, your body either prepares to fight perceived danger or gears up to run away from it. Your heart rate increases, stomach production shuts down, hormones are secreted, pupils dilate, and breathing rate speeds up.

A simple way to recognize when you are struggling emotionally is to check your breathing. If you are experiencing negative emotions, you will tend to breathe more quickly and shallowly, in the upper half of your chest. The simplest way to calm down this fight-or-flight reaction is to practice deep breathing. It is so simple, yet it unleashes a powerful calming response.

Ideally, sit in a comfortable place without crossing your arms or legs. Place one hand on your chest and one hand on your stomach. The goal is to take in full, deep breaths, making sure that your stomach rises.

You might want to close your eyes. Breathe in slowly for a count of five, hold for five seconds, and then release slowly on a count of five. Go through this at least five times. Don't be surprised if the first time you try this, you feel a little dizzy and uncomfortable. This is just your body readjusting. You may also notice that sometimes you hold your breath when you are stressed. The more you practice this technique before you get stressed, the lower your overall stress level will be, and the less likely it will be for your emotions to escalate as quickly.

If you were ever to catch me in traffic with my kids arguing in the backseat, you would see that I had one hand on the wheel and one on my stomach. I would be practicing deep breathing so I don't crash into the idiot in front of me or get involved in the sibling fight behind me.

Practice the deep-breathing exercise now. After going through several cycles, what did you notice before and after you did it?

_____

_____

_____

E—EXPAND: expand your awareness to your entire body and the area around you. Pay attention to your surroundings and how they make you feel. Identify any triggers that you are facing. Think through what would happen if you stayed in this environment and what would happen if you took a drink.

This process is called a body scan. It is a mindfulness exercise where you focus on what you are feeling in your body. I find it helps to go through several cycles of deep breathing, then do a body scan.

Notice what thoughts are running through your mind. You don't have to do anything about them; just observe them as if they were words floating by. Do you feel any stress or tension in your head or face, your neck, or shoulders? What is going on in your stomach? How does your back feel? Are you clenching your teeth, hands, or jaw?

Mindfulness is about noticing, not necessarily reacting in the moment. When we learn to be present in the moment, we can manage our emotions better. Once you have expanded your awareness, this often kicks in the parasympathetic nervous system, the one that relaxes the body and calms down the fight-or-flight response. Next, you can evaluate with your logical, not emotional brain.

If you are experiencing negative physical symptoms, take a moment to determine whether you could take action to address them. If you are feeling excitement, happiness, or relaxation, celebrate that feeling and figure out how you can repeat and increase it in a healthy way!

Practice doing a body scan. What did you notice before and after?

_____

_____

_____

R—RESPOND: the goal is to respond, not to react. A reaction tends to be emotional, while a response is more intentional. To respond mindfully means you are aware of both your internal and external experiences and are making a conscious choice of what to do about them. Once you know what is going on in your mind and body, you can take the appropriate steps. Realize that sometimes you may not know what you are feeling or what to do. This is a great time to call someone in your support system or to post on a moderation forum and get some perspective. We often make things worse in our own heads, but the people who know and love us can offer a different perspective, bring us back to reality, help us make decisions, and provide support.

It is important to identify who you can call before you need them. They should be able to give you support and perspective. I encourage you not only to reach out when there is a problem but to keep regular contact. Often, they can pick up on shifts in your mood and behavior, warding off a problem and preventing it from being a full-blown crisis.

Don't make the mistake of waiting until there is an issue, not wanting to "burden" anyone. You deprive others of feeling needed and useful if you never reach out for support. They will also be more likely to reach out to you when you have a reciprocal relationship.

Who can you talk with to help you respond better?

_____

_____

_____

Reducing Risky Situations

Traditional treatment says that people experiencing problems from alcohol must give up all people, places, and things associated with drinking. I have a different approach. I focus more on _levels of risk_ because sometimes we are unable to avoid them completely. Sometimes the people are our family, and the places are our homes or places where we must go in our day-to-day lives. When we look at life in terms of black and white, we often give up because an all-or-nothing approach is unrealistic and too hard to maintain. I prefer to explore the shades of gray. I want you to know your risky people, places, and things and consider your levels of risk associated with them.

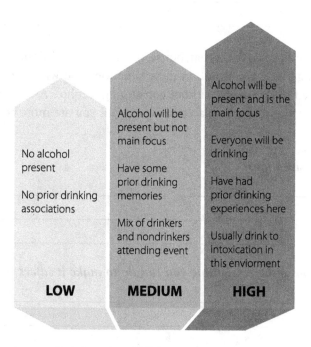

Image 7.1 Levels of Risk

LOW RISK: Alcohol is unlikely to be at this event, the people in attendance are not regular drinkers, and you have no past associations of alcohol here. I encourage you to stay in low-risk situations as you are going through a period of abstinence and when you begin practicing moderation. I recommend having a plan before attending the event or location. Make sure the people you are going with know your current drinking goals and either bring a nonalcoholic beverage or have your nonalcoholic drink choice in mind before you get the question: Can I get you a drink?

What are your low-risk situations?

_____

_____

_____

MEDIUM RISK: Alcohol may be present at this event, but it is not the main focus. You may have consumed alcohol at this place in the past, but you also have nonalcohol-related memories of it and know people there who will not be drinking. This is a situation that you could attend, but you should have a plan and go with a support person who is aware of your goals and challenges.

What are your medium-risk situations?

_____

_____

_____

What can you do to make them safer?

_____

_____

_____

HIGH RISK: You know that if you go to this bar, house, party, concert, casino, club, or sporting event, etc., drinking will be taking place. You drank in these situations and with these people in the past. You have never participated in this event without consuming alcohol. As you are readjusting drinking patterns, high-risk situations may be places to avoid until you are more confident and comfortable with your new plan.

What are your high-risk situations?

_____

_____

_____

Should you avoid them, or is there anything you can do to make it safer?

_____

_____

_____

Bill's friends had one of the funniest ways of dealing with risky situations:

Bill was a self-admitted pickle who drank to excess, had received several DUIs, blacked out frequently, and had lost things that were important to him, including his marriage and license to drive a car. He participated in a recovery program that included detox, individual therapy, dual-diagnosis group therapy, and regular support group attendance.

One of Bill's closest childhood friends was getting married. The best man planned to have the bachelor party in Las Vegas. Bill's friends did not have an issue with alcohol; binge drinking was the main agenda. Bill's friends wanted him to go on the trip so badly that they offered to pay for a prostitute to stay with him to make sure he did not drink when they were out!

Bill realized that this trip was too high of a risk for him, and he decided not to go. He skipped the bachelor bacchanal but happily attended the weekend events for the wedding. He recently celebrated five years of sobriety.

DID YOU KNOW? Many DUIs occur in the morning hours. The average body processes alcohol at a rate of .016 BAC per hour. This is why it is generally safe to have one drink per hour and still be able to drive. However, you must consider the amount and the number of hours you have been drinking. People try to be responsible after a night of heavy drinking by deciding to stay where they are rather than drive. However, when they wake up in the morning, their body is still processing the large amount of alcohol they consumed. They may not feel impaired, but the alcohol is still in their system. If they drive and are pulled over, they may register a high Breathalyzer reading.[55]

Urge Surfing

Another goal in the early months of alcohol abstinence is developing self-regulation skills through mindfulness techniques. This is learning how to tolerate negative emotions and delay rewards. G. Alan Marlatt is credited with the concept of "urge surfing."[56] The idea is that cravings are like waves, and breathing is like a surfboard that carries you through the wave. We can use deep breathing to ride out the wave (craving).[57] I find this is helpful because it acknowledges that the desire to drink can be powerful, but that there is a simple technique that you can use anywhere, anytime (breathing). Because urge surfing can be visualized, you can also see that an urge is not permanent. It may peak but will eventually dissipate, as waves do.

Just because we have a thought or feeling does not mean we have to indulge it. Distraction is another healthy way to manage cravings. Develop a list of healthy distractions to have in place prior to needing it. Knowing what to do in a crisis can help you feel more prepared for what to do when you are having a craving. Remember all those fire drills you participated in as a child?

You are more likely to follow through with activities that you come up with, but sometimes we need help developing ideas. Alcohol has likely been a part of your life since you were a teenager, so it can be hard to remember what you enjoyed. Here are some of the more common things that can be done alone. They do not require transportation or significant amounts of money:

_____ Listen to a podcast
_____ Read a magazine
_____ Call a friend
_____ Play a computer game
_____ Watch a television show
_____ Listen to music
_____ Journal
_____ Pray
_____ Meditate
_____ Take a walk
_____ Do your nails
_____ Take a bath
_____ Organize something
_____ Lift weights
_____ Do housework
_____ Reach out to your support person
_____ Play with your kids
_____ Surf the internet
_____ Attend a self-help meeting
_____ Tune into the game
_____ Read recovery literature
_____ Review online moderation tools
_____ Post on a moderation forum
_____ Watch a yoga video on YouTube
_____ Look up funny animal videos
_____ Say the Serenity Prayer
_____ Watch a TED Talk
_____ Read a novel

_____ Prepare a meal
_____ Leave a message for your therapist

Which distractions will you try?

_____

_____

_____

What are five others that you could do?

_____

_____

_____

If none of them work, what can you do? This may require going someplace else or meeting with someone in person, like your support person or a therapist.

_____

_____

_____

Coping With Cravings

If you are experiencing a craving, ask yourself the following questions:

What am I feeling physically?

_____

_____

_____

Pay special attention to your head, neck, and stomach. These are the places where you will often experience the physical outlet of emotions. Explore what happened right before the urge. What does the urge want? If it could speak, what would it say to you right now? Is it trying to tell you something about yourself?

What am I thinking?

_____

_____

_____

You may experience a rush of many different thoughts. Pay attention to any self-defeating patterns. Take several deep breaths and imagine any negative thoughts being placed into the cargo hold of an airplane. Imagine the negative thoughts and patterns flying away so that you can focus on healthy, positive thoughts and patterns. The more senses you engage in a positive thought or image, the less able you are to think about the negative one.

Where do you feel most happy, safe, and comfortable? Recall what you see, hear, feel, and smell.

_____

_____

_____

It helps to bring up a location that you have been. When you think about this place, your brain remembers the positive feelings and elicits the positive emotions associated with it.

Dealing With Triggers

A trigger can increase an urge to drink. I recommend not judging it as "good" or "bad." I view it as an opportunity for change.

Emotional: this is how you feel. Often people acknowledge only negative emotions like sadness, loneliness, depression, and anger. However, positive ones like confidence, satisfaction, and excitement can also cause a relapse. Many times people use alcohol to celebrate the completion of a goal or a task.

What are your triggers related to negative emotions?

_____

_____

_____

What are your triggers related to positive emotions?

_____

_____

_____

Physical: this refers to what your body feels like. Do you reach for a drink to alter your physical state? You may drink to help you relax, manage stress, or feel numb. Regular drinkers are often used to having a quick fix that alters their mood and physical state quickly. Be aware that there is very little that will work as quickly as alcohol did. But a benefit to using other tools is that there may be fewer consequences to them.

What are your physical triggers?

_____

_____

_____

People: it sounds like a cliché, but there are people whose actions may make you want to drink. It may be because others around you are all drinking and you feel like you are missing out. Or you may have a negative history with someone, so you drink to deal with hurt, anger, or resentment. While no one can control you, other people certainly can influence you.

Which people contribute to your wanting to drink?

_____

_____

_____

Availability: there will be alcohol present. Sometimes it is obvious like at a bar, sports event, wedding, or party. You may need to avoid these events for a period of time because adequate willpower and coping skills have not yet been developed. Alcoholics Anonymous has some great sayings when it comes to being around alcohol: "If you stand by the buffet table long enough, you're going to eat"; "Hang around a barbershop a while and you're going to get a haircut"; or, "Wait in line at the hot dog stand, you're going to eat a hot dog."

In what situations is alcohol regularly available in your life?

_____

_____

_____

Social pressure: if I am around these people or this situation, I will feel like I am expected to drink and will be an outcast if I do not. This trigger is like a combination of people and availability.

When do you feel social pressure?

_____

_____

_____

Memories: I have strong, positive recollections of drinking in these situations and it is hard to remember any consequences. This is where I teach the concept of "play it through 24."

What memories tend to elicit alcohol-related memories?

_____

_____

_____

Play It Through 24

One way to deal with the triggers and cravings is to "play it through 24." The idea is to identify what would happen if you took a drink. It gets you out of just the momentary pleasure and considers the long-term reactions. Think through the following:

What will happen in the next 24 seconds?

_____

_____

_____

What would happen in the next 24 minutes?

_____

_____

_____

What can occur in the next 24 hours?

_____

_____

_____

What about the next 24 days?

_____

_____

_____

Image 7.2 Play It Through 24

It is important to recognize that the chemical effects of alcohol are powerful. This is why people drink. The first one may feel good. You may experience an initial relief, soothing, or relaxation. However, if you think about the next 24 minutes, you recognize that you may not stop at one or two and begin to stop caring about the consequences. Playing it through the next 24 hours, or even 24 days, can help to identify what your alcohol goals are. You may realize that the consequences outweigh the pleasure. The trick is to know how many drinks this is for you. For some, one is too many, and the end of the bottle is not enough. For others, having several occasionally keeps them in a healthy zone.

At this point, it may still seem like I am advocating for complete abstinence. I recommend only going through a period of time. Based on your experience, you can then determine what your relationship with alcohol will look like. While the tools listed in this chapter are more appropriate for achieving sobriety, they can still be used to monitor the effectiveness of ongoing alcohol moderation.

Are you ready to move on to the major part of this book: the *Alcohol Moderation Assessment*? It gives you predictions about your ability to successfully practice alcohol moderation.

Chapter Eight
Taking the *Alcohol Moderation*
Assessment

This chapter is the essence of this book—the *Alcohol Moderation Assessment*. You can take it and then read on for the interpretation of your results.

Interpreting the Assessment

Answers to the *Alcohol Moderation Assessment* predict the likelihood that you will be successful in practicing alcohol moderation. While some of the questions relate to your early development, refer to the last six months of your life when thinking about your responses. Checking "yes" on the first 17 questions are negative predictors for successful moderation. You will notice that some of them are not specifically related to alcohol consumption but are environmental risk factors. Answering "yes" on any of questions 14 to 17 usually mean that you are unlikely to be able to practice alcohol moderation. These questions have to do with how your body has been affected by alcohol and are often signs of alcohol dependence. The last three questions are protective factors. These are attributes that help individuals deal with stress and decrease the chance of a negative outcome. Please see the following interpretations for each of the questions.

   1. Do I have more than two drinks a day for men/one for women? As noted in previous chapters, women who have more than one drink a day and men who have more than two are considered to be moderate drinkers. The larger the amount and the more frequently you drink, the harder it is to change your pattern. Drinking every day is a negative predictor. If you associate drinking with specific events, it may be more challenging to moderate drinking. If nights and weekends signal drinking time, it will be very important for you to develop new associations.

ALCOHOL MODERATION
ASSESSMENT

PLEASE ANSWER **YES** OR **NO** TO THE FOLLOWING QUESTIONS:

		YES	NO
1.	Do I have more than two drinks a day for men/one for women?		
2.	Has my alcohol use been increasing?		
3.	When I drink do I have a hard time stopping?		
4.	Do I have any medical issues?		
5.	Am I taking any medication?		
6.	Have there been repeated consequences from my alcohol use?		
7.	Have I experienced trauma or have a PTSD diagnosis?		
8.	Am using alcohol to change my mood?		
9.	Has my alcohol use negatively affected my loved ones?		
10.	Do I have any mental health concerns?		
11.	Do I use any other non-prescribed mood altering substances?		
12.	Do I have any legal, probationary, or work issues?		
13.	Was I raised in a heavy drinking environment?		
14.	Have I had withdrawals from drinking?		
15.	Do I have elevated liver enzymes?		
16.	Have I experienced blackouts?		
17.	Was my first drink before age 15?		
18.	Will I review my alcohol use with my support system?		
19.	Do I have alcohol-free outlets or hobbies?		
20.	Am I willing to go through a period of abstinence?		

Image 8.1 *Alcohol Moderation Assessment*

ALCOHOL MODERATION
ASSESSMENT

SCORING THE ALCOHOL MODERATION ASSESSMENT

- For questions one through thirteen, give yourself one point for any "yes" answers.

  POINTS: _____

- For questions fourteen to seventeen, give yourself two points for any "yes" answers.

  POINTS: _____

- For questions eighteen to twenty, subtract a point for any "yes" answers.

  POINTS: _____

Total your points. The amount reflects your likelihood of being able to successfully practice alcohol moderation.

TOTAL POINTS: _____

< 0 Points	Good
1-5 Points	Fair
6-10 Points	Poor
>11 Points	Unlikely

Image 8.1 (Continued)

Julia is someone who was able to change her lifestyle to be able to drink at safer levels:

Julia was in her 50s, worked full-time, and was now helping raise her single daughter's six-year-old son. On top of that, her father's health was declining, and he had to be moved into a nursing home. Julia was at the end of her rope. She found that martinis were a great way to deal with her stress. However, she noticed that she was going to the liquor store so often that the clerks there greeted her by name. In addition, her daughter told her that her grandson had begun asking why Grandma acted funny at night.

Julia decided that she couldn't eliminate any of her responsibilities, so she needed to find other ways to deal with her stress. She joined her local gym and discovered yoga, as well as two other women who were dealing with similar life struggles. Together they picked at least one weekend day a month for a girls' day, took turns babysitting each other's grandkids, and went to lunch after visiting their parents so they could vent about their stressors.

Julia was not a lifelong drinker. Although she had begun drinking every day, it was due to situational stressors. Once she found other ways to manage the stress, she realized that she did not need the outlet of alcohol every day. Julia cut down her drinking to having martinis only when she went out for dinner. She is now enjoying more energy in the morning, no heartburn at night, and feeling more joy in her relationships.

2. Has my alcohol use been increasing? Refer back to Chapter 3, where we reviewed how to diagnose substance use disorders according to the *Diagnostic and Statistical Manual of Mental Disorders,* 5th edition (DSM-5). The first of the criteria was "Alcohol is often taken in larger amounts or over a longer period than was intended." For many, this process creeps up over time. No one starts out polishing off a bottle by themselves or drinking the entire 12-pack. The amount and frequency of alcohol use can increase over a period of years. A typical process is this: An individual may have a glass or two of wine a couple of times at social events. They find that they like the effect, so they bring a bottle home and start having one with dinner. A waiter is not pouring it so the standard pour of five ounces becomes eight or nine ounces at home. One glass becomes two servings. Over time they do not get the same effect from one glass, so they begin having two or three, which is actually three to four servings, putting them in the category of heavy alcohol use. This process is called tolerance.

Tolerance refers to criterion number ten: Tolerance, as defined by either of the following:

a.   A need for markedly increased amounts of alcohol to achieve intoxication or desired effect.
b.   A markedly diminished effect with continued use of the same amount of alcohol.

Tolerance is especially dangerous when it reaches the point of physical addiction—when the body will go through a withdrawal process if it does not get the substance.

3. When I drink, do I have a hard time stopping? You may have heard the term "One is too many and ten is not enough." This refers to the person for whom once they start drinking, it is very hard to stop. For some individuals, they do not stop drinking until the alcohol is finished, they pass out, or everyone goes home. Some individuals cannot fathom how others can leave some of their drink unfinished. This type of drinker often consumes all liquids, including nonalcoholic beverages, quickly. They don't sip; they swallow in quick succession.

Other drinkers seem to "reach a point of no return" or "flip a switch." This typically has to do with the physiological effect of alcohol. When most individuals reach a blood alcohol concentration of 0.04–0.06, they become relaxed, have lowered inhibitions, become more talkative, and have impaired judgment. This often takes only two to three drinks for most people.[58] This is another reason why it is important to stay within moderate drinking guidelines. People around this type of drinker will often say "One moment you were fine and the next it was like there was a different person."

Some individuals recognize this point of no return and can decide not to cross that line. They stop drinking. Others may be consuming alcohol so quickly that the psychological effects also hit quickly, and they lose their ability to make good judgments because alcohol has impaired them.

Answers to this question also relate to the second DSM-5 criterion: "There is a persistent desire or unsuccessful efforts to cut down or control alcohol use." You may realize that you are losing control over your ability to control your intake. You may not yet be ready to admit it. This is why it is important to review the assessment with a trained professional, a trusted loved one, or someone whose feedback can be heard.

4. Do I have any medical issues? This question and the next question have to do with the ninth DSM-5 criterion: "Alcohol use is continued despite knowledge of having a persistent or recurrent physical problem that is likely to be exacerbated by alcohol."

There are some obvious all-or-nothing predictors related to medical conditions. The most common include pregnancy, cirrhosis, elevated liver enzymes, diabetes, or cancer. There are many others that should be discussed with your doctor. Additionally, if you have high blood pressure, high cholesterol, or a weakened immune system, you probably are not a candidate for moderate drinking.

Chapter 4 reviewed how alcohol affects every organ in the body. Although the health risks associated with heavy drinking can take years to develop, they also can make current conditions worse. I recommend an open conversation with your doctor so that you can make an educated decision on the amount of alcohol, if any, that is acceptable for your health.

5. Am I taking any medications? There are contraindications for drinking with many medicines and supplements. Some medications, when taken with alcohol, can intensify drowsiness and put you at risk for accidents, falls, and even death. These may include medications for heart disease, insomnia, pain relief, and colds, as well as medications for psychiatric conditions like depression, anxiety, bipolar disorder, ADHD, and schizophrenia. Alcohol interactions can also occur with over-the-counter medicines like antihistamines, pain relievers, cough medicines, and some herbal preparations. Alcohol is known to affect antibiotics, antidepressants, antiseizure medications, benzodiazepines (for anxiety), opiates (for pain), and beta-blockers (for heart or high blood pressure).

This medication list is by no means exhaustive. Please check with your doctor, psychiatrist, or pharmacist to determine the impact of alcohol on any medications you are taking. Many psychiatrists report that alcohol mixed with antidepressants reduces their effectiveness. Make an educated decision on whether it is safe to drink and take certain drugs. Be aware that a combination of alcohol and some drugs, such as sleeping medications, benzodiazepines, and certain medications for depression can have lethal consequences. I always recommend taking prescribed medications instead of taking a drink.

6. Have there been repeated consequences from my alcohol use? This question refers to DSM criteria five, six, and seven:

- Recurrent alcohol use resulting in a failure to fulfill major role obligations at work, school, or home.
- Continued alcohol use despite having persistent or recurrent social or interpersonal problems caused or exacerbated by the effect of alcohol.
- Important social, occupational, or recreational activities are given up or reduced because of alcohol use.

Some consequences are hard to deny, such as a legal charge, loss of a job, or the end of a relationship. However, some of the consequences can be more subtle. Denial causes people to minimize what happens when inebriated. If you always seem to end up in a physical fight with your brother, engaged in a debate that leads to screaming, passed out snoring on the couch, or if someone else always seems to end up crying, it may be a good idea to look at alcohol's contribution to the problem. Only you and the people closest to you can determine if your drinking is a problem. As I said previously, if it causes a problem, it is a problem.

This is where self-assessment is really important. It can be hard, but it is very important to seek the observations and opinions of the people closest to you. If you have heard the same concern from someone more than once, it may be valid. If you have had the same complaint from a number of people, it is likely true. It may be hard to hear, but feedback from others can let you know what it is like to be on the receiving end of your actions.

The drinker in this relationship did not feel there were problems with his drinking, but his partner did:

William and his partner James had been together for over ten years. He and James would often go out to the clubs and imbibe in the nightly specials. After several years of working hard, they were able to purchase a house that they turned into their home. William still preferred to go out, but James liked to stay in.

The couple often hosted monthly dinner parties. William was the social butterfly, always with a drink in his hand and a story to tell. However, William and James had begun fighting more, especially about William's going out. James was concerned about the money he was spending, how late nights were affecting his health, and the risks of driving home. His trust in his partner was decreasing, and their sex life took a turn for the worse. Not as many friends were attending their parties. William would often get loud and rude after a few drinks, James was then left making apologies and cleaning up after everyone.

Alcohol misuse is not always as obvious as a DUI, a loved one ending a relationship, or health issues. Drinking can affect the quality of your relationships. Intimacy may decrease, fights may occur, and ongoing tension can damage your overall happiness.

7. Have I experienced trauma or have a PTSD diagnosis? Experiencing trauma is one of the main predictors for having a substance use disorder. In one survey of adolescents receiving treatment for substance use, more than 70% had a history of trauma exposure.[59] Teens who experienced physical or sexual abuse were three times as likely to use substances than those who have not.[60] And 59% of young people with post-traumatic stress disorder (PTSD) develop substance use disorders. Another study found that 60% to 80% of Vietnam veterans seeking PTSD treatment have alcohol use problems. They tend to binge drink in response to memories of trauma.[61] Another study reports that approximately 8% of the population will develop PTSD during their lifetime. There is a strong correlation between experiencing trauma and developing a substance use disorder.[62]

People who suffer from trauma and PTSD often turn to alcohol and other drugs to manage the intense flood of emotions and traumatic reminders. They may also use it to try to numb themselves. Drugs and alcohol initially dull the effects that they are experiencing from the trauma and help them manage the distress. But a dangerous cycle may begin.

After a traumatic event, people may drink to deal with anxiety, depression, and irritability. But it may be the worst thing to do. Alcohol initially seems to relieve these symptoms. When we experience a traumatic event, our brains release endorphins that help numb the physical and emotional pain of the event. This is our body naturally helping us cope. These endorphin levels eventually decrease over the next several days. Consuming alcohol actually increases our endorphin levels. Sounds good, right?

However, this interrupts the natural protective function that the body was already doing. As a result, we create a type of emotional withdrawal that can set us up to deal with increased and prolonged emotional distress that could even lead to the development of PTSD.[63]

Drinking often can increase PTSD symptoms and increase irritability, depression, and feeling off guard. Some drink to deal with insomnia that results from anxiety, anticipating nightmares, and circular thinking. However, drinking actually impairs the quality of sleep, setting you up for a never-ending cycle.

If you are using alcohol, you may be less able to cope with a traumatic event. You will have increased difficulty with emotional and behavioral regulation. Also, the earlier age that your drinking starts, the more your emotional development gets impaired. As a result, you may be more likely to engage in risky behaviors that can actually lead to additional trauma.

The combination of trauma and drinking issues increases the challenges of getting close to people and having conflicts with the people that you do have a relationship with. Heavy drinking often leads to a confused and disorderly life. The very thing you need is support and connection, yet those are often damaged as a result of your drinking.

8. Am I using alcohol to change my mood? It is important to understand why you drink. There are many possible reasons. If it is to escape from feelings or an unpleasant situation, this is a negative predictor. It will be important to develop coping skills to deal with any underlying psychiatric issues like depression, anxiety, obsessive-compulsive disorder, or insomnia. If you are drinking to avoid problems in a relationship, job, or living situation, it is time to evaluate the environment. See if acceptable changes can be made to the situation, or examine whether it is time to leave a job or a relationship. Therapy can be very helpful in working through these issues.

Lee is an example of someone who learned how to drink in moderation, even though he struggled with mental health issues:

Lee was a 51-year-old entrepreneur. He was intelligent, successful, and had all the trappings of success that a man could want: beautiful wife, three healthy children, and enough money to take several vacations a year. But he could not seem to get a handle on his depression. He would use alcohol to deal with feelings of sadness and worthlessness.

Lee scared himself the night he drove home after a business meeting and could not remember how he got there the next morning. He spent the next several months in individual therapy, addressing issues that had haunted him from childhood. Because he was still struggling with symptoms, he also sought the help of a psychiatrist to find the right antidepressant that significantly reduced his symptoms without causing serious side effects.

Lee chose to go through a period of abstinence from alcohol. During this time he developed better coping and communication skills, but he really missed wine. He was one of the rare people who could tell the difference between a $10 bottle and a $100 bottle. He developed an Alcohol Moderation Plan that allowed him to drink his favorite wines only in social situations and never more than two glasses at a time.

If Lee noticed the frequency of his drinking increasing, or if his depression symptoms began affecting his day-to-day life, he first talked it over with his wife. Lee trusted her opinion, and she was able to give support without criticism. If he did not feel better within two weeks, he would schedule an appointment with me to come up with strategies to help him feel better again.

Again, if you drink to change your mood, it is a negative predictor. If you have alcohol as part of a holiday or social gathering and are not trying to change your mood or emotions, it is a more positive predictor. Even better is if you appreciate a fine wine that brings out the flavor in food, enjoy a cold beer on a summer day, savor the flavor of an aged liquor, or relish making a toast with champagne. Successful alcohol moderators see alcohol as part of the event, not the main event.

"Successful moderators see alcohol as part of the event, not the main event."

9. Has my alcohol use negatively impacted my loved ones? If drinking is causing problems in your primary relationships, you may have to decide which is more important to you. Parents also need to be aware of messages about alcohol you are sending to your children. Do you want your children to have the same relationship with alcohol that you do? Realize that kids are like sponges. Parents set the example for what is normal because you are the primary adults in their lives; what their children see them do is imprinted on their brains as normal. All other experiences will be compared to their early first observations and impressions.

If your children are adolescents, they may begin to experiment with alcohol. Be wary of "Do as I say, not as I do." You will lose your credibility. The teenagers I see in my adolescent dual-diagnosis program report little respect for parents who yell at them for going to a party and drinking, while they are holding their own glass of alcohol and slurring their speech from a few too many.

Sid is a good example of someone who decided to change his drinking patterns as a result of how it affected his family:

Sid was a 74-year-old father of two and grandfather of five who was looking forward to celebrating his golden anniversary with his wife. He admitted that when he was in his 30s, he had a problem with alcohol. As a result, he became a regular AA participant and even sponsored new members. After several years, he stopped attending meetings, believing he had heard and said it all.

After almost 20 years of sobriety, Sid wondered if he finally had this thing licked and could be "normal" again. To Sid, "normal" meant that he could drink like most people, without consequences and able to stop with one or two glasses. However, when Sid drank, it was in secret. One of his favorite places to drink was in the car. It gave him a double adrenaline rush. After a few months and too many close calls, he realized how dangerous this was for him and confessed to his wife. He decided to stop drinking liquor but still had the occasional glass of wine.

Sid never became intoxicated again, but every time his wife or kids saw him with alcohol or smelled it on his breath, they were triggered and remembered the misery of his earlier years of heavy drinking. Sid decided that his family's happiness and well-being were more important to him than drinking. They just celebrated their 50th anniversary, and they toasted each other with sparkling cider.

10. Do I have any mental health concerns? The likelihood of having both an AUD and a mental health disorder is very high. The 2014 National Survey on Drug Use and Health found that there are about eight million people in the United States who have an AUD as well as a mental health disorder.[64] If you struggle with depression, bipolar disorder, anxiety, schizophrenia, post-traumatic stress disorder, or obsessive-compulsive disorder, and you drink, this is a negative predictor. However, once these issues are stabilized, you may be better able to explore whether moderate drinking is an option for you.

The National Alliance of Mental Illness (NAMI) notes that drinking can be a way of self-medication—that is, people seek the effects of alcohol as a way to make their symptoms less painful.[65] However, alcohol can actually worsen underlying mental illness while the person is under the influence or during withdrawal from alcohol. Drinking can make symptoms of depression worse and increase panic attacks, not only from the actual chemical use but also from the consequences of drinking. Additionally, alcohol use can trigger the onset of psychosis.

As noted earlier, it is critical to address any mental health issues before trying to drink moderately. This can be done in a variety of ways. It may be by developing better coping skills, getting out of a bad relationship or situation, seeking appropriate medication, resolving issues with a therapist, developing meaning in some form of spirituality, or learning new ways to relax and have fun. There is no quick fix and no one answer. You will likely need to address many areas, but any investment should result in a healthier, happier version of life.

11. Do I use any nonprescribed mood altering substances? The use of any other nonprescribed mood-altering substances (drugs) is a negative predictor. As noted previously, if you use a substance in order to change your mood, you are likely to remain in that pattern.

John's ongoing marijuana use shows how he is not a good candidate for alcohol moderation:

John was a single 33-year-old alcohol and marijuana user. He had decided that his drinking was causing him a lot of problems. He had developed quite a beer belly, suffered from high cholesterol and high blood pressure, and had to take medications for them. He wanted to be in a relationship but had no motivation to meet anyone new.

When John realized that most of his paychecks were going to beer and weed, he decided to get some help. He began therapy. His group members offered him great support and accountability, but he was reluctant to address his marijuana use. He said it was a natural substance and smoking it did not have any negative effects on him.

Six months later, John was abstinent from alcohol but still smoked pot several times a week. He held the same hourly-paying job, played video games for fun, and had no significant other. He couldn't figure out why nothing had changed. Had he stopped smoking marijuana, he might have had a better chance to evaluate his life and been more proactive in his life goals. Because he was still using a mood-altering substance, he was unable to gain enough clarity to fully evaluate his life.

12. Do I have any legal, probationary, or work issues? These are obvious negative predictors. If your freedom, driver's license, or job is on the line, you should not keep drinking. Once the probationary period has passed, developing an Alcohol Moderation Plan can be explored.

13. Was I raised in a heavy drinking environment? There is no one specific gene that determines if you will have a problem with drinking. Hundreds of genes in your DNA can influence the likelihood of developing an alcohol-related problem. Genetics appear to be responsible for about 50% of our risk of developing an issue. You will be about four times more likely to have an AUD if you have a direct family member such as a parent or sibling who has an issue.[66]

While our genes are responsible for half of our likelihood of developing a problem, the other 50% is due to our environment. As noted previously, the people who raise us and the atmosphere we live in shapes our sense of what we think is normal. If you were raised in a family where alcohol was a part of daily living, your outlook will be impacted by this. When alcohol is seen as the way to celebrate, socialize, deal with stress, or end the day, people develop skewed perceptions. Adult children of alcoholics (ACOA) are three to four times more likely to develop a problem with drinking. This is often due to the chaotic environment, neglect of physical and emotional needs, and poor boundaries.[67]

Negative Predictors

The next four questions are very negative predictors for alcohol moderation. This is why the scoring adds two points for each affirmative answer. If you experience these, you may have a severe AUD with a physical addiction. It is unlikely that you will be able to successfully practice alcohol moderation. When your body becomes physically addicted to alcohol, willpower and behavior modification are often ineffective.

14. Have I had withdrawals from drinking? The final DSM-5 criteria address withdrawal.

Withdrawal, as manifested by either of the following:

a. The characteristic withdrawal syndrome for alcohol (see the following).
b. Alcohol (or a closely related substance, such as a benzodiazepine) is taken to relieve or avoid withdrawal symptoms.

If you have experienced delirium tremens ("the shakes") or a seizure, you are often not able to safely drink again. If you have had hallucinations or delusions (seeing or hearing things that are not there), these are serious symptoms that are very negative predictors for being able to drink moderately.

Remember that tolerance to and suffering withdrawal from alcohol indicates a severe drinking issue. There is consequently much less of a chance that you can keep drinking safely or moderately. It is possible but comes with very high risk. You should evaluate why continuing to drink is so important. I recommend speaking with a therapist trained in addiction treatment and moderation to help make this very important decision.

DID YOU KNOW? Withdrawal from alcohol can kill you. Many people mistakenly believe that coming off painkillers, stimulants, or heroin can be fatal. It generally is not. These withdrawals are extremely painful, with the acute symptoms lasting for several days, possibly up to a week. Alcohol is a central nervous system depressant. CNS depressants, often referred to as sedatives or tranquilizers, slow brain activity. This is why when you drink, you feel more relaxed and do not filter your thoughts, actions, or words as well. When a person no longer has alcohol in the body, the CNS begins to experience a rebound effect that can result in potentially life-threatening complications related to the heart, breathing, seizure, kidney, or liver.[68]

15. Do I have elevated liver enzymes? As described in Chapter 4, alcohol can destroy the liver. Heavy drinking causes inflammation, fatty deposits, and scarring. When your liver is damaged, it can no longer perform its metabolizing jobs, thus allowing toxic substances to travel to your brain.

One way to tell if your liver has been damaged by alcohol use is through a liver enzyme test, also known as a liver function panel. I recommend that anyone who has consumed alcohol on a regular basis and wants to attempt alcohol moderation get their liver enzymes checked. It is a simple blood test that can be ordered by any doctor. There are even at-home test kits that involve a finger prick.

The test shows the number of enzymes that are flowing out of your bloodstream due to cell damage.[69] If these are elevated, I caution you against trying moderation. If you still want to try, I suggest you do compete abstinence for six months and then repeat the test.

I caution you about starting and stopping heavy drinking. The liver is one of the only organs that can regenerate. This sounds great. However, if you consume alcohol on a repairing liver, it is extremely dangerous. The new cells are very sensitive and are more likely to become damaged at a faster rate.[70]

16. Have I experienced blackouts? If you have had more than one blackout, this is a negative predictor for continued use of alcohol. There are two kinds of alcohol-related blackouts.

The first is associated with binge drinking. Binge drinking is defined as drinking several drinks (four for women, five for men) within a two-hour period that elevates the blood alcohol level to 0.08 or higher. This type of blackout may occur once or twice before the individual learns his or her limits and decides not to make the same mistake again. This is often seen in the teenage or college drinker who consumes a large quantity of alcohol in a short period of time. In addition to injury, fighting, and sexual assault, this type of blackout can seriously impair learning and memorization—typically a major role function for young adults in college or learning a trade.[71]

The other type of blackout, which is more concerning, typically occurs on a more regular basis in the heavy drinker.[72] The large amount of alcohol consumed prevents the brain from forming long-term memories, and the drinker loses a period of time. This is not forgetting a few things you said last night, but losing a few hours, not remembering things you did or how you got home. This is extremely dangerous because you may take risks that you normally would not, such as taking other drugs, going home with a stranger, or driving a car while impaired.

A blackout indicates brain damage. Alcohol is preventing your brain from encoding experiences and turning them into long-term memories.[73] If you have had repeated blackouts, it is a negative predictor for your ability to moderate drinking. For most people, a safety valve will turn on, and they will do one of several things when they drink excessively. They will consciously decide to stop consuming drinks, pass out (fall asleep), or throw up. Most people do not and are not able to drink to the point of having a blackout.

17. Was my first drink prior to age 15? Beginning to drink before the age of 15 is a strong negative predictor. One study of over 40,000 adults found that nearly half of the people who began drinking before the age of 15 met the criteria for a severe AUD. That percentage dropped to less than 10 percent if they waited until age 21.[74]

Researchers at the National Institute on Alcohol Abuse and Alcoholism (NIAAA) believe that alcohol more negatively affects younger teens' brains because they are not yet fully developed. Alcohol can lead them to make choices that focus more on immediate pleasure versus making choices that avoid the long-term impact that heavy drinking can bring.

In addition to the legal reasons, there are biological reasons to delay drinking until the age of 21. Current research tells us that the brain is not fully developed until, on the average, age 26. This is significant because of a process called cell adaptation,[75] which refers to the changes made by a cell in response to adverse environmental changes. In other words, if a substance is introduced into a developing brain, the brain cells believe they need this substance to continue developing. If an underdeveloped brain is given alcohol, it will adjust and continue to need more and more of it to grow. This is what we call tolerance. Tolerance to alcohol is a negative predictor for the ability to moderately consume it.

The example that follows shows how delaying drinking can help be a positive predictor for alcohol moderation:

Jorge was a shy young man. In accordance with his cultural upbringing, he lived at home until he was in his late 20s. He had saved up enough money and now wanted to see what it was like to live independently.

Jorge moved to a new area, but he was very shy and struggled to make new friends. He found that going to happy hour at bars was a good way to meet people. He learned that after five or six drinks, his social anxiety disappeared and he could openly talk with anyone. This worked great until he got pulled over for a DUI.

While Jorge's drinking pattern classified him as a heavy drinker (having several binges a month, drinking more than five drinks at a time, and drinking multiple nights a month), he had not yet developed a tolerance to alcohol. This was likely due to the fact that he had delayed drinking until he was 28 when his brain was fully developed. Because his prefrontal cortex—the area of the brain that is last to develop and is responsible for thinking, memory, and judgment—was mature, he eventually realized that there were other, healthier ways to meet friends, and he found better ways to deal with his social anxiety.

One day Jorge took a risk and struck up a sober conversation with a neighbor. Together they participated in other nondrinking activities that allowed him to develop better social skills, which reduced his fear of talking to new people. He still goes to the occasional happy hour but no longer feels the need for the social lubrication. His new girlfriend and wallet are happy that he no longer is a regular at the local bar.

Protective Factors

The next three areas have to do with protective factors. They are behaviors that increase the potential for successful alcohol moderation.[76] The assessment has you subtract one point for every affirmative answer.

18. Will I review my alcohol use with my support system? Research shows that one of the most positive predictors of success for your ability to moderate your drinking is having a good support system.[77] There are many reasons for this. One is that people with a good support system tend to be happier and have lower rates of mental health issues. A support system also helps you stay accountable. When you look in the eyes of someone you love, they can often feel your guilt, and you want to be a better person for them.

This is why the best weight-loss programs include some form of accountability, which in turn leads to more goals achieved. If you have to share a food journal with a nutritionist, you are more likely to think about what you put into your body. And the scale does not lie—it knows when you have had too many chips or cookies. The same can be true with keeping a drinking diary that you share with your support system. Writing how often, how many, and the impact of your drinks can be very telling.

Think about who in your life has what you want. Identify those qualities and figure out how to emulate them. Find a mentor who helps with increasing honesty, tracking goals, and finding solutions. This may be a friend, loved one, parent, online support group, therapist, spiritual leader, or fellow alcohol moderator.

Honesty is crucial. Your support system should have a copy of your Alcohol Moderation Plan, which will be discussed in the next chapter. Give them permission to challenge and confront you as well as celebrate successes. Your support person should be strong enough to handle your resistance and give you guidance.

19. Do I have alcohol-free outlets or hobbies? Alcohol often becomes a way to relax and have fun. It is important to develop activities that do not involve drinking. You will have more success if you add something that you enjoy rather than just focusing on avoiding alcohol. We do better when we have an enjoyable outlet rather than a deficit

20. Am I willing to go through a period of abstinence? As noted in Chapter 6, before trying moderation, I recommend being alcohol-free for a period of four months. Studies have shown that those who go through a period of abstinence are more likely to reach their alcohol-related goals.[78]

One of the main reasons is to handle a wide variety of situations without alcohol. During this time, you may experience some discomfort. The goal is to identify triggers and learn other coping skills. Being chemically free helps bring your emotions to the surface, thus giving you an opportunity to manage life in a different way.

When thinking about being alcohol-free, you may focus only on negative emotions such as anxiety, stress, depression, boredom, and anger. You may be pleasantly surprised at the emergence of positive feelings that perhaps had been numbed by alcohol: joy, awe, love, compassion, and empathy.

Additionally, you may have fallen into unhealthy patterns. This period of abstinence allows you time to break them. Drinking or not drinking becomes less of an issue when your attention, time, and activities are on other opportunities. I recommend saying "I choose not to drink" rather than "I can't drink." The former implies empowerment rather than deprivation.

What were the results of your assessment?

_____

_____

_____

What do you need to address before developing your Alcohol Moderation Plan?

_____

_____

_____

Chapter Nine
Alcohol Moderation Tools

This chapter will describe some of the most common alcohol moderation tools and how you can put them into practice. They are grouped in topics that include: blood alcohol concentration, physical, emotional, environmental, tracking, and motivational.

Blood Alcohol Concentration

Know Your BAC

Successful moderators know the effects of their blood alcohol concentration (BAC). It is the percentage of alcohol in your bloodstream. Alcohol is classified as a sedative or depressant substance because it impairs or "slows down" mental and physical functioning. For the average person who does not have a physical dependence on alcohol, these are the most common effects of a rising blood alcohol level:[79]

0.02%–0.039%: Most drinkers begin to feel the effects of alcohol and experience slight euphoria, loss of shyness, and relaxation.

0.04%–0.059%: There is a feeling of well-being, relaxation, low inhibitions, and warm sensations. You start to have some impairment of judgment and memory. Feelings of euphoria emerge. You get more talkative and confident.

0.06%–0.99%: Balance, speech, vision, reaction time, and hearing is slightly impaired. There is reduced judgment and self-control. Reasoning and memory are impaired.

0.10%–0.129%: There is a significant impairment of motor coordination and judgment. Speech is slurred. Balance, peripheral vision, reaction time, and hearing are all impaired.

0.130%–0.159%: You have gross motor impairment and lack of physical control. Vision is blurred and there is a loss of balance. Euphoria is decreasing and you begin to feel unwell.

0.160%–0.199%: You feel nauseous and act sloppily.

0.200%–0.249%: You need assistance walking and are mentally confused. You may vomit and experience a blackout.

0.250%–0.399%: Alcohol poisoning is occurring. You may lose consciousness, have a seizure and irregular and slow breathing, blue-tinged or pale skin, low body temperature, and an inability to be awakened. This is a medical emergency that can lead to brain damage or death.

0.40%: Onset of coma and potential death due to respiratory arrest.

While there are increasingly depressant effects on the body, most people experience an initial stimulating effect. In lower doses, alcohol increases arousal but with ongoing consumption, alcohol reduces energy and awareness. You feel good initially with the first drink or two, but the effects become more impaired and dangerous over time. This is why most moderation programs recommend keeping your BAC below 0.06.[80]

Your BAC can be measured in breath, urine, or blood. If you want to know what your BAC is, you can purchase a Breathalyzer for less than $100 online or in most drug, electronics, or big box stores. These will be less sensitive than what law enforcement uses.

Your BAC will range based on a number of factors. The more you weigh, the more fluid you have in your body, the more the amount of alcohol gets diluted, thus having less of an effect. Therefore, the less you weigh, the more quickly alcohol will affect you. Women tend to have higher BACs for the same amount of alcohol as a man consumes. Women also generally have higher percentages of fat and therefore less water in their bodies to dilute the alcohol.

Pace and Space

The idea of "Pace and Space" is to have no more than one drink per hour and to space your drinks out over a period of time. Simply putting the beverage down in between sips can help you pace yourself. If a drink is in your hand, you are more likely to drink it. Pacing and spacing also refers to having a nonalcoholic beverage in between alcoholic drinks. I encourage having a glass of water for every alcoholic drink, although you may prefer soda, juice, or tea.

Dilute Your Drink

Another way to prevent your BAC from rising as rapidly is to dilute your alcoholic beverage. Simply adding extra ice, including more nonalcoholic mixers like soda, or reducing the amount of liquor in a mixed drink can all help. Instead of drinking straight liquor, have it on the rocks. Or make a spritzer out of wine. Just be cautious of drinks that are more flavorful, as you can wind up drinking more.

Rotate Nonalcoholic and Alcoholic Beverages

Rotating between a nonalcoholic beverage and one containing alcohol helps in several ways. It helps you pace yourself and prevents your BAC from rising too quickly. Alternating beverages also prevents the dehydration that alcoholic beverages can cause, which may lead to hangovers.

Sip Slowly and Mindfully

When drinking, sip slowly and mindfully. Some people eat and drink quickly, causing digestion problems, overeating, and overdrinking. If you drink quickly, the effects hit faster, making it harder to pace yourself. This is why drinking straight liquor and doing shots can be risky because the alcohol goes into your bloodstream rapidly. If you sip slowly, you can savor your drink. You may find that you don't actually like how alcohol tastes and realize you were only drinking for effect. Alcohol is a high-calorie beverage. Make sure that you are enjoying it.

> **DID YOU KNOW?** Drinking coffee, going for a walk, or taking a cold shower will not help you sober up. On average, it takes two to three hours for a single drink to leave the body. Nothing can speed up this biological process.[81]

Know Your Point of No Return

Some also call this the "F**k-It point" when they appear to have no off switch. Most people reach this point around a BAC level of 0.06%. At this point, you are unable to determine if you have had enough. For most, this is two to three drinks.

Physical

Satisfy Physical Needs First

Alcohol cravings may be a sign that your biological needs are being unmet. Prior to taking a drink, you should first satisfy your physical needs.

- Are you hungry? When we experience low blood sugar, we become irritable, impatient, anxious, and shaky. All of those can mimic a craving.
- Are you thirsty? Early signs of dehydration can include hunger pangs, fatigue, and headache. Many people consume beverages loaded with caffeine, like soda, coffee, and tea, which have a diuretic effect.
- You should identify if you are tired. This too makes people irritable and reduces willpower and judgment.

You should not take a drink if any of these three areas are not addressed first.

Eat Before You Drink

Alcohol is absorbed into your bloodstream from your stomach and small intestine. If you do not have any food in your stomach, the alcohol will go directly into your bloodstream, causing your BAC to rise faster, and you to feel the effects more rapidly. It helps to drink nonalcoholic beverages to dilute the alcohol in your stomach and slow absorption.

Emotional

Pay Attention to Your Urges

An urge is the desire to start or continue drinking. People, places, situations, events, and emotions all can be triggers. Once you identify your urges, you can develop a plan of how to cope. Sometimes it may be to best to avoid the situation that leads to urges, and sometimes you just need a plan to manage an urge when it occurs. This can include leaving the situation, calling a friend, reviewing a list of why you chose to change your drinking patterns, etc.

Do Not Drink When You Are Upset

Alcohol is a depressant. While you may initially experience feelings of relaxation, warm sensations, and lowered inhibitions, in larger doses it affects judgment, reasoning, memory, and self-control. Alcohol typically magnifies your emotions. For example, if a person drinks when he or she is angry, the alcohol will reduce that person's inhibitions, and he or she is more likely to get into a physical altercation. If that person is upset about a breakup, a few drinks will alter his or her judgment and that person may have casual sex with a stranger, only to regret it in the morning.

Alcohol is known to reduce the effectiveness of many medications. Regular alcohol use also interrupts neurotransmitters that are needed for regulating our mood.[82] It narrows your perceptions so that you do not respond to cues around you. If you are prone to anxiety, you will be on higher alert. If you struggle with depression, you may interpret the world around you even more negatively.

My clients report that when they use alcohol to change their mood, they often feel worse for several days afterward. Keep in mind that when a substance gives an emotional lift, there will be a converse reaction with an even worse mood as a result. In the long run, you can be on a never-ending cycle where you are trying to recover from the last emotional dip. Your baseline mood lowers every time you drink until depression is your baseline state.

Unpairing

In the initial small doses, alcohol releases the feel-good chemicals of opioids and dopamine. However, the "placebo effect" also occurs. We believe alcohol is doing something so we feel something. You may notice an instant feeling of gratification as soon as you grab a cold beer or feel relaxed as soon as you take your first sip—long before any alcohol has reached your bloodstream to cause any effect. I want you to know about what I call "unpairing."

You may associate the pleasurable effects of alcohol with the action of drinking. It became your way to relax, celebrate, have fun, end the day, reward yourself, etc. I want you to think about what drinking equals for you. This is also like understanding your "why." Once you recognize your associations, you can look at other ways to achieve the desired effect. Just as the pairing can be developed, it can be undeveloped. Some common pairings include:

Beer = the end of a day
Wine = my reward
Champagne = celebration
Cocktail = party

What are your alcohol pairings?

_____

_____

_____

What could a new association be?

_____

_____

_____

Remember that over a third of the population does not drink alcohol at all, and the majority can take it or leave it. I remind you of this because you may struggle to imagine situations or events in which people do not drink. Most of my clients notice that when they go through the period of abstinence, they were the one who was encouraging alcohol to be present. Sometimes they also realize that a lot of their friends and situations involved alcohol and may need to change some of their people or places.

Environmental

Never Drink Alone

Drinking alone often indicates that you are trying to change your mood, which is a negative predictor for moderation. While you certainly can get out of control when you are around others, being around people can be a type of check. If practiced mindfully, you can see your behavior reflected in the people around you. Explore if you are drinking more or less than others. Pay attention if people are sipping their drinks or doing shots. Notice if others are becoming intoxicated and determine a plan to safely get home. A successful Alcohol Moderation Plan (discussed in the next chapter) identifies in greater depth what a safer drinking plan will look like.

Don't Keep Alcohol in the House

We tend to eat or drink what we have easy access to. If there is no alcohol in your house, it creates a small speed bump where you have to get dressed, leave the house, and go to a store, bar, or restaurant to get a drink. Having to make a trip gives you a few minutes to think about whether you really want a drink or if something else will satisfy your craving. If it is in the house, you are less likely to think it through. Some keep alcohol in the house for guests, but I recommend that when you have people over, buy just enough and then send any leftovers home with them.

Drink Only in Social Situations

My most successful alcohol moderators drink only when there are other people around, as part of a social event. They do not make drinking the main focus.

Only Consume Alcohol During the Event

Don't drink before or after the event, only during. Some people consume alcohol prior to the event to calm their nerves before entering the social situation. Explore why this anxiety is occurring, see if this is a signal that you should not attend, and come up with conversation starters ahead of time. You are not a young adult anymore and don't need to "pre-game"!

Pick a Nonalcoholic Drink

Identify a nonalcoholic beverage that you enjoy on a regular basis as well as one when you want to be more festive. Some of my clients find they manage fine at home but then feel like they are missing out when they attend a celebration where others are drinking. Many alcoholic beverages can come in the form of a "mocktail." These are what some call beach or boat drinks but do not have any alcohol in them. You can order a virgin margarita, piña colada, mojito, etc., and still feel like you are on vacation or celebrating. Mocktails can be quite elaborate and include exotic fruits and other mixers with fewer calories and consequences.

Craig worked in the restaurant industry for most of his life, so drinking was a big part of special occasions for him. One day in a therapy session, he was lamenting that he would be celebrating his birthday during his period of abstinence. He had always looked forward to hanging out with the regulars and having them buy him a drink rather than making one for them. Given that he had bartended for years, I suggested he create a "mocktail," a nonalcoholic mixed drink. I could see the wheels turning in his mind as we ended the session.

The next week, he came in proudly for two reasons. One was that he had celebrated his birthday alcohol-free, finally sticking to his commitment after many failed attempts. And two, he had created a new mocktail that was going to be added to the restaurant's menu and named after him!

Rehearse a Response

You may associate "drink" with an alcoholic beverage. What about water, soda, tea, juice, or coffee as a drink? Regular drinkers who become abstinent or change their drinking patterns are often worried about how other people will react to their decision or how to answer the question of what to drink. Think back to the last social gathering you attended. How much did your best friend drink, your significant other, your coworker, neighbor, etc.? This reality testing process can help you realize that you are putting more attention on what you are consuming than others likely are. It may feel like there is a spotlight on you, but there usually is not.

Prepare a short response for how to handle the question, "Would you like a drink?" It may be helpful to tell a close friend or family member that you have changed your drinking patterns so that they can run interference for you. For example, if your in-laws are big drinkers, ask your spouse to talk to them to make sure there are no uncomfortable moments, or bring your own drink and have it in your hand so that you avoid altogether the question of what to drink.

Below are some statements that others have found helpful:

- "No, thank you."
- "I'm doing a cleanse."
- "No, I'm not pregnant; I just feel like having water."
- "I'm saving my calories for dinner."
- "Alcohol and I no longer mix."
- "I'm trying to lose this belly."
- "Not drinking is my New Year's resolution."
- "I'm giving up alcohol for Lent."
- "Oh, I've already got something."
- "I'm the designated driver."
- "I'm doing a challenge."

- "My doctor wants me to lose a few pounds."
- "I'm on probation."
- "I'm watching my sugar level."
- "My doctor is monitoring my A1C levels."
- "It makes me sick."
- "I've had my share."
- "I don't drink anymore."

Humor works well to put everyone at ease. Additionally, you can always speak the simple truth or order a non-alcoholic beverage. Use the one-liner you are most comfortable with. Practice saying it out loud before you arrive at your destination. In this way, you will feel more prepared when you are confronted with a drinking situation, thus avoiding an awkward moment for you as well as your host. If you set the tone of being relaxed and comfortable, the people around you will respond positively. You may also want to devise a signal with the person you are with to let them know when it is time to go. I also suggest this for friends and couples who just want to go home early!

What response works for you?

_____

_____

_____

Avoid High-Risk Situations

If you have always consumed alcohol in that situation, at that place, or with those people, they should be avoided. Focus not on what you may lose, but what you can gain. When we are giving something up, we feel deprived. This is why I encourage you to make a list of what has happened when you were in high-risk situations. You may realize that the consequences were not worth the short-term fun or that you can adapt the situation so the outcome is different.

Avoid Heavy Drinkers

If you plan on consuming alcohol, anticipate the environment. When you are around people who are drinking heavily, you are more likely to go with the flow and keep pace with them.

Be the Designated Driver

There are times when you do not feel you can miss a high-risk situation. Examples include a work event, a friend's wedding, a family member's birthday, an annual event, or a holiday gathering. In these situations, it can be helpful to offer to be the designated driver. Most people respect this and do not continue to offer alcohol. Many bars and restaurants will offer free nonalcoholic drinks to the person who is driving.

I have worked with a number of clients who were consistently nominated by their peers to be the designated driver because they were abstinent. After feeling used and seeing how intoxicated their peers were getting on a regular basis, many decided to establish new peer groups and different ways to socialize.

Plan an Early Event for the Next Day

Planning an event for early the next day can help when you will be in risky situations, when you are sticking to a reduced amount, or are not drinking. When you have something to look forward to in the morning, you will feel less like you are missing out. Additionally, it gives a good reason for why you are drinking less or remaining abstinent.

Focus on the Conversation, Activity, or People

For successful moderation, the situation should not be about the alcohol but participating in the surroundings. You may feel uncomfortable the first time you go when you stop or reduce your drinking, feeling like all eyes are on you, wondering what is wrong and why you are not drinking. This is why it is important to have a statement prepared, have a support person, know your levels of risk, understand and deal with your "why," etc., prior to attending a drinking situation. After going once or twice with your new relationship with alcohol, you will realize that most people are having their own internal conversations, focusing on themselves and their experiences. However, if after going to the same type of event with the same people, you are still feeling uncomfortable, it might be time to reevaluate your social circles and how you spend your time.

Tracking

Accountability Partner

Bringing an accountability partner when drinking is helpful in several ways. Communication and trust are important. You should communicate your goals to them. That person needs to be willing and able to step in if you are not sticking to your plan. Their job is one of support, not probation. If you need someone to count drinks and say when to stop, you are not ready to be practicing moderation.

If you go to an event on your own, you can check in with a friend before and after the event. They can help you predict risky situations and follow up on how you managed the drinking situation.

Use a Daily Counter

This can work for both abstinence and moderation. Get a calendar and hang it in a prominent place in your house. For each day that you either have a day of not drinking or drinking within moderation guidelines, you put a check on the calendar. The counter helps you stay accountable and is a visual way to track your success. The calendar also helps you see if there are patterns. It is especially helpful when you use a full annual calendar to see if there are patterns during certain times of the year, like holidays, seasons, birthdays, or annual remembrances. Having others see this tangible reminder is another way to get support, motivation, and accountability. Seeing the positive checks also helps to regain trust from family members.

Keep a Drink Diary

Paying attention to when you drink, how much you drink, and how you feel before and after drinking is helpful. The drink diary gives you data. By writing this information down, you may start to see patterns. You may realize that whenever you spend time with a certain group of people, you tend to overdrink; or you may find that your willpower is not as strong when you are under a deadline; or that you thought you had a certain amount a week, but when you see it on paper, you realize it was more.

Avoid Back-to-Back Drinking Days

There are numerous reasons not to consume alcohol on a daily basis. By not drinking every day, you are more likely to reduce the amount you drink, reducing the overall health risks. Having off days from consuming alcohol requires you to have other tools for managing stress, relaxing, having fun, ending the day, etc. It also helps you to avoid getting into a habit. If you do the same behavior every day, it can be very easy for the amount of alcohol to increase.

Drink Tracking

When practicing moderation, you can use physical reminders to track drinks. Women can put on the corresponding amount of bracelets or rings for the drinks they plan to have and then move them to the other hand once the drink was ordered. Men can wear their watch on their opposite wrist as a way to be conscious when consuming alcohol. The brain notices when things are out of place and can help you be more intentional.

There are hundreds of apps that assist you with tracking your alcohol consumption. Nearly everyone carries a smartphone with internet access. An app can convert and track intake quantities of alcohol consumed, send an alert when a limit is reached, track how much money is spent or calories consumed, send inspirational messages, or set off an alert when you go into a risky geographic boundary.

Set an Alert

In addition to drink tracking, you can use your phone for moderation support. You can set an alert to go off at a predetermined time when you plan to leave an event. This should be prior to the point of intoxication, when your judgment is not impaired and you are less likely to ignore the alert. Most people report that at a certain point in the evening, people have become loud, annoying, and obnoxious. When you drink less, you may realize that you no longer enjoy those types of events and do not feel like you are missing out on anything.

Motivational

Tangible Reminders

I recommend using tangible reminders—things you see, feel, touch, and hold—that remind you of why you are making changes to your drinking patterns. Identify something you want more than alcohol. Often this has something to do with your loved ones, your health, financial situations, material possessions, or goals. It helps to make it personal.

Some positive reminders may include the following:

- A picture of the house you want to buy with your loved one if you resolve the problems related to your alcohol use.
- The car you want to drive once your license is reinstated.
- A photo of your kids on your last vacation when you were sober and got up early to play with them on the beach.
- A mug from the school you want to attend or the place you hope to work.

Motivational reminders could include:

- Putting a sticky note of the Serenity Prayer on the dashboard of your car.
- Keeping a clean-date countdown on your phone.
- Listening to a recovery related podcast each day.
- Reviewing an inspirational quote each morning.

While most of us are more motivated by positive reminders, remaining aware of the consequences of drinking is very important as time passes and we forget how bad it was. These are some of the negative tangible reminders that you can try:

- Keep the business card of your therapist or probation officer where you will see it before you open your wallet to pay for alcohol.
- Place the bracelet from your last hospital stay after your accident in the area where you keep your wine or highball glasses.
- Write down all the reasons you changed your drinking patterns, and review them the next time you experience a craving.

Glass Jar

Another tangible reminder that I recommend includes a technique I call the Glass Jar. Get a glass container. The reason for the glass is so that you can see the contents. I encourage you to put it in a common area of your home so that not only do you see it, that your loved ones see it as well.

Then calculate how much you typically spend on alcohol in a given day: perhaps $20 on a bottle of wine or $60 on your bar tab. Next, identify something that you would like to treat yourself with: a massage, a round of golf, clothes, a designer purse, or tickets to a game. Then go to go to the bank and get $10 bills in the amount of what your treat would cost. For each day or situation that you do not have a drink or stick to your moderation goal, put the amount of money you would have spent in the container. For every day that you do not stick to your plan, take double the amount out of the container. At the end of a designated period of time, you can use the cash saved by making better choices to enjoy your special treat.

Many find that this is a great tangible representation of how much they were spending on alcohol and how making small choices every day can add up to something positive. You may also think twice when you know that overdrinking will cause you to lose double your savings.

Create New Traditions

Alcohol has likely been present for many events in your life. It may be hard to imagine New Year's Eve without champagne, a sports event without beer, a holiday dinner without wine, a cigar without bourbon, or a vacation without a cocktail. I want you to develop new traditions.

Focus more on a new side dish for your holiday dinner instead of wine. Save the calories that you would have consumed on alcohol for a second helping or more dessert. Try the Spanish tradition where you eat a grape for every strike of the bell at midnight instead of a champagne toast. When doing a toast, there is no rule that it has to be an alcoholic beverage. You can still raise a glass no matter what is in it. For a sporting event, have a competition on who makes the best chili, wings, or dip instead of downing beers. You may find that you actually enjoy the event more when you are not constantly running to the bathroom, don't get into fights, or have a hangover. For other celebrations, focus more on the activities. During get-togethers, concentrate more on fitness and have a competition or race instead of waiting until the afternoon and looking forward to the open bar. Or try a high adventure activity to mark a celebration. Try ziplining, spelunking, rock climbing, whitewater rafting, swimming with sharks, or skydiving where alcohol is typically not present.

Healthy Transitions

For many, alcohol signals the end of the day or a reward for a job well done. Transitions are important to signal to our brain and body that it is okay to "turn it off." This is again why I encourage a four-month period of abstinence.

Courtney was someone who learned transitions other than alcohol:

Courtney was in sales. She telecommuted for one of the major tech companies and was always pushing to meet her quotas. As soon as she woke up, she turned on her computer. Throughout the day the email notifications pinged constantly. If she got hungry enough between cups of coffee, she would silently shove some microwaved food in her face while on yet another conference call. This went on all day until her husband asked if she was coming to bed. She would down a few glasses of wine to "shut it down."

Courtney's situation is common for many people. She worked from home so her brain never had time to transition from work to home mode. She was always "on." Additionally, Courtney was not eating well, artificially energized herself with numerous cups of coffee, and had stopped working out to be on calls in other time zones. She thought that the alcohol was helping her wind down and fall asleep. She was at her wit's end and willing to try something different. Courtney had gone to a few AA meetings but did not feel she fit in there.

I first educated her about sleep hygiene. Modern society is having more issues with insomnia and it is related to artificial lighting, especially what is emitted from our phones, pads, and computer screens. The light interrupts the body's production of melatonin, a natural hormone that affects sleep. Melatonin traditionally falls in the morning and rises in the evening. Artificial light blocks its production. The length of time in front of her screens and continued use into the evening was negatively affecting her sleep.

Courtney had been a tennis player in college, so she knew about the importance of healthy proteins, fiber, and micronutrients. She was opting for convenience rather than quality in her food, always chasing the next commission.

As she began eating more whole foods, her energy level increased so she did not need to rely on coffee throughout the day. She also took a short break to eat, finding that fueling her body, clearing her head, and changing scenery actually increased her productivity more than pushing straight through. Early in her period of abstinence, her quantity of sleep improved. She also realized that she had been in a never-ending cycle: she was constantly working, drinking to relax and induce the onset of sleep, then having poor-quality sleep that affected her mood and motivation. She did not have the energy to see how much of a toll her job was taking on her. While she earned a high income, she realized that she did not have the time to enjoy it. Ultimately, she decided that a job change to a local company made more sense. Creating healthier transitions has allowed her to make time to enjoy dinner with her husband and resume her passion for playing tennis.

Identify Natural Highs

What did you enjoy doing as a child? Get back to doing those activities! Remember the days where you would spin in circles just to get a different feeling? Didn't you go outside and play? You did not have to have a plan; you could make an adventure out of a stick and a rock. Often, people forget how much they once enjoyed the outdoors. Do you like to hike? Fish? Animal watch? Look at the stars? Stare at the water? Most of these are free and can be done alone or with people.

If you enjoy feeling a rush, try skydiving, mountain biking, white water rafting, kayaking, ATV riding, or ziplining. If you are competitive, get involved with sports, enter a race, raise money for a cause, or volunteer. Prefer a slower pace? Listen to music, read, cook, explore the arts, do yoga, Tai Chi, or Pilates.

Develop a List of 100 Things to Do Before I Die

Everyone should have one of these lists. Research has shown a variety of benefits from participating in novel and arousing experiences. When we do something that is different and exciting, the brain releases the feel-good neurotransmitter called dopamine.[83] This improves the quality of our long-term relationships.[84] New experiences also reduce the cognitive decline of aging.[85] Your List of 100 Things to Do Before I Die should be big goals that may take time to complete, like earning a degree, speaking another language, developing a skill, or traveling abroad. There should be easily achievable goals like trying a new food, seeing a certain movie, or visiting a local attraction. I also encourage a variety of activities that include adventure, travel, skills, experiences and include work, spirituality, and relationships.

Review

Determine a time to periodically review the successes and failures of your drinking habits. If you are having trouble moderating alcohol use, you might need to go through another period of abstinence. Or you may come to the realization that abstinence works better for you. If the suggestions and tools presented in this chapter appear punitive, you may not be ready to try alcohol moderation. Moderation Management says it best: Take Responsibility. Acknowledge that drinking is something you do, not something that happens to you.[86]

Which tools are ones that you want to try?

_____

_____

_____

Chapter Ten
Developing an Alcohol Moderation Plan

Prior to developing an Alcohol Moderation Plan, you should have completed the following. Place a checkmark next to the ones you have done:

- ☐ Received education about the impact of drinking.
- ☐ Understand your "why."
- ☐ Have not developed a physical dependence on alcohol.
- ☐ Know the moderate drinking guidelines for your gender.
- ☐ Can commit to not engaging in unsafe behavior after drinking.
- ☐ Do not misuse other mood-altering substances.
- ☐ Do not act in self-destructive ways after drinking.
- ☐ Experienced a period of abstinence.
- ☐ Identified triggers and made a plan to deal with risky situations.
- ☐ Experienced a range of emotions and learned how to cope with them.
- ☐ Determined that it is safe to continue drinking.
- ☐ Know alcohol moderation tools.
- ☐ Chosen a support person to review.

Were there any that you did not complete? What do you have to do to make sure it is taken care of?

_____

_____

_____

Ideal Use Plan

After making sure each of the areas above is addressed, one of the first steps in creating an Alcohol Moderation Plan is to answer this question:

If you could have your ideal drinking plan, what would it look like?

_____

_____

_____

From this, we can work backward into your plan.

Alcohol Moderation Plan

What follows is a sample Alcohol Moderation Plan:

ALCOHOL MODERATION PLAN

I am choosing moderation because: _____

_____

_____

I will not drink in these situations: _____

_____

_____

I will not drink until: _____

_____

_____

I will not drink after: _____

_____

_____

I will alternate an alcoholic beverage with: _____

My non-alcoholic drinks are: _____

I will have no more than _____ drink/s per: _____ For a total of: _____ Per: _____

I will review my plan with: _____

If I/we notice: _____

_____

_____

I/we will: _____

_____

_____

Signature: _____ Date: _____

Support Person: _____ Date: _____

Image 10.1 Alcohol Moderation Plan

An explanation of why each of the components is listed on the Alcohol Moderation Plan is as follows:

I am choosing moderation because: This is another chance to explore your "why." Answers that are similar to those listed are positive predictors of success for the plan: I enjoy wine with my meal, I want to socialize with my friends, I like having a few beers during the game, I enjoy a cocktail on vacation, or I'd like to toast to our success at the end of a project. These are all specific and add to a social situation but are not the main focus. If you are still looking to change your mood, want to become intoxicated, or are unhappy without drinking, you are unlikely to be able to practice successful alcohol moderation.

> "If you are still looking to change your mood, want to become intoxicated, or are unhappy without drinking, you are unlikely to be able to practice successful alcohol moderation."

_____

_____

_____

I will not drink in these situations: Identify times when you will not consume alcohol at all. These typically correlate to your risky situations and may include certain people, places, and things. These also should include areas where you have experienced problems in the past, safety reasons, and concerns expressed by loved ones. The safety ones tend to be the easiest to identify and may include: "I will not drive if I have had any alcohol," "I will not have alcohol if the kids are with me," "I will not do shots," etc. Be careful about minimizing problems from the past. As time passes, we tend to forget their impact.

Developing a successful Alcohol Moderation Plan involves your loved ones. You should be aware of their areas of concern and have a plan for how to address them.

My most successful alcohol moderators do not drink on back-to-back evenings, drink only in social situations outside of their home, and generally do not drink more than once a week. Many include not drinking on back-to-back days, even during a holiday weekend or vacation.

_____

_____

_____

I will not drink until: Remember that the Dietary Guidelines for Americans state that if alcohol is consumed that it should be in moderation: up to one drink a day for women/two for men. While the National Institute on Alcohol Abuse and Alcoholism states that low-risk drinking is defined as no more than three drinks on any single day for women/four for men and no more than 7 a week for women and 14 for men. Given these low amounts, alcohol consumption should be relegated to the event. I recommend against drinking at home.

Most people's plans will state that they will not drink until they are at the event, game, party, wedding, restaurant, etc. Some go further to state that they will not order a drink until they have eaten or had a nonalcoholic beverage first. When we are hungry or thirsty, we tend to eat and drink more rapidly. Sports fans write that they will not drink until after the first quarter, inning, or period.

Many note that "day drinking" leads to serious consequences for them as they start early and go all day. Therefore, people designate a time of day like after work, chores are completed, dinner, kids go to bed, the weekend, etc.

I've worked with many retirees who have had challenges with increasing alcohol use. When there is no schedule and reduced responsibilities, they have to be more on guard. One gentleman was used to not drinking until he was finished with work. When there was no more employment, he found he was drinking earlier and earlier in the day. Another person stated that he would not drink until the sun went down. This worked well when we created the plan in June, but I had to help him decide what how to adjust in the winter months.

_____

_____

_____

I will not drink after: This area identifies times and situations when you will commit to not drinking. For example: "I will not use alcohol if I have had a fight with my significant other," "Once the event is over, I will stop drinking," or "I won't continue drinking after getting home." You may also want to designate a time when you will stop consuming alcoholic beverages like past 9:00 p.m. or after my spouse gives me the signal. This can be a tricky area if there is still tension between significant others. It works best once the drinker has earned back trust, has involved them in the moderation process, identified warning signs, and mutually agreed on a signal if your drinking is getting out of control. Couples may have a predetermined gesture, like placing a hand on their partner's back, or a statement that signals that it is time to stop drinking.

_____

_____

_____

I will alternate an alcoholic beverage with: As has been previously reviewed, successful moderators keep their blood alcohol concentration below 0.06, which is where impairment typically begins. This is often around two drinks. In order to slow rates of consumption and absorption, you should have both food and liquid in your stomach. By switching between a nonalcoholic and an alcoholic beverage, you can prevent your BAC from rising too quickly. This is especially helpful if you will be at an event for several hours at a time

_____

_____

_____

My nonalcoholic drink is: I find that this is one of the easiest, yet most commonly overlooked moderation tools. People need to find a nonalcoholic, "special occasion" beverage. Many nondrinkers report that they feel left out of the celebration because they are not drinking alcohol. When they are at home, they are fine drinking soda, tea, coffee, or water but struggle when they are in a social situation. I encourage them to pick a beverage that they would not have on a regular basis. Maybe this is a sweet tea, a flavored coffee, regular soda, tonic and lime, or sparkling water garnished with fruit. Remember how fun it was to get a Shirley Temple as a kid? It's amazing how festive a cherry and a little grenadine can make one feel. Adults often need to re-program themselves that an alcoholic beverage does not equal celebration.

_____

_____

_____

I will have no more than _____ *drink/s per:* _____ *For a total of:* _____ *per:* _____ . These numbers are going to depend upon your gender, weight, and tolerance. Males and those who weigh more can consume more alcohol with fewer effects. Regardless, I still recommend no more than one drink per hour. You also need to note the total amount you plan to consume in a setting and in a week. I recommend that women should have no more than two to three drinks in a setting, while men have no more than three to four. Any more than these amounts is considered a binge.

You need to identify alcohol's effect on yourself. If you have gone through the recommended period of abstinence, your tolerance level may have decreased, and thus you will be affected by lower amounts of alcohol. My most successful moderators stick to one to two drinks for women and two to three for men and not more than once a week. Most report that they begin to feel the effects after two drinks and have a harder time staying within their limits. Those who drink more than two also report that they notice an effect the next day.

_____

_____

_____

I will review my plan with: Choose a person who will show support as well as accountability. This is often a significant other. Issues of trust should have been resolved. If your partner is still having concerns, it is not time to try moderation. Both partners should have good communication with each other. Any accountability should not be punitive. It should come in the form of noticing if you are sticking to your Alcohol Moderation Plan, pointing it out if there is some slipping, and discussing what to do as a result. The person is more of a partner than a probation officer. Their statements should be more along the lines of: "I noticed . . ." than accusations.

It is important to assess whether the support person is able to fill this role. They should be willing to participate in the process. They do not have to be alcohol-free, but they should have a healthy relationship with alcohol. If you remember the description of donuts who drink within moderation from Chapter 3, they often make the best support people. Cucumbers and pickles who are currently struggling with their alcohol use are unlikely to be able to offer support. Waters, those who do not drink alcohol at all, also may not be good support people as they may not understand the desire to drink and struggle to cut down.

_____

_____

_____

If I/we notice: You and your support person should identify warning signs that the plan is not working. Areas that are typically included are on the Quick Check described in the next chapter. It includes the amount, frequency, intent, and impact of alcohol use.

_____

_____

_____

I/we will: Determine what you and your support person should to do if the areas above are observed. Identify the best way for them to confront you if you deviate from your plan. They may say something like: "I notice that you are drinking more frequently than you said you wanted to on your plan. You agreed that if that happened you would take a break for a month."

Many people include going through another period of abstinence if they are not sticking to their plan. This may be for a shorter time, like 30 days to recalibrate. Some check back in with their therapist. Others commit to participating in an online forum, journaling, or getting more information through reading or listening to podcasts. It is helpful to plan ahead for risky situations. Some also develop a situation-specific moderation plan, like for a vacation or special event like a wedding.

_____

_____

_____

DID YOU KNOW? There is a way to test for alcohol use from three to four days prior. A Breathalyzer, urine screen, or blood test measures how much alcohol is in your system. There is a new test that measures the amount of ethyl glucuronide (ETG) in your system. ETG is a direct metabolite of the alcohol that you drink and remains in the body even after the alcohol itself can no longer be detected. The presence of ETG in urine indicates recent alcohol consumption, often up to 80 hours.[87]

It can also help to review your patterns. Is there something that stands out? Do you overdrink whenever you go to a certain place or are with specific people? Are you not managing your mood? Or did life circumstances change like switching jobs, getting sick, or having children? Not following through on the plan is not a failure; it means that something was not working and needs to be adjusted. A good support system will help you rework your plan, not responding with anger or withholding affection. If the subtle changes are caught quickly and renegotiated, these issues are less likely to arise.

What are my patterns?

_____

_____

_____

Signature, Date, and Support Person: Include the signatures of both you and your support person as well as the date. This takes the form of a contract that people take more seriously. Both of you have made commitments, and both of you are witnesses to it.

_____

_____

_____

Fill out your plan and make sure the people in your life know what is on it.

While this is a contract, your Alcohol Moderation Plans is not written in stone. The plan should be a fluid document that adapts as your life changes. Just be wary of making so many exceptions that they become habits. Both of you should be involved in any updates to the plan. The next chapter reviews how to monitor its success.

Chapter Eleven
Monitoring Your Alcohol Moderation Plan

There are a number of terms people use when they talk about returning to problematic alcohol use: relapse, lapse, slip, or reoccurrence. Some call a "slip" or a "lapse" an incident of drinking outside of the limits you set in your Alcohol Moderation Plan, while a relapse is going back to a pattern of drinking outside of your plan. I define relapse as a process of thoughts, behaviors, patterns, and emotions that can lead back to the original problem. The most important word that I want you to remember is process. It is not an event; it's a progression that is typically observable and therefore, preventable. When you have a plan for how to observe the process, you can course correct faster and reduce consequences. Listed in this chapter are several of the tools you can use with use to prevent lapses from progressing to relapses:

Quick Check of Alcohol Moderation Plan

A simple check to evaluate if your Alcohol Moderation Plan is working effectively is the Quick Check:

Amount

Keep in mind the guidelines for the amount and frequency of alcohol consumption. For men, that means no more than 14 drinks a week, and for women no more than 7 a week, and not all at the same time. Remember that recent studies have shown that no amount of alcohol is considered safe or healthy. Your job is to determine what you safe level is. I have found that the people who experience the greatest success with alcohol moderation usually drink no more than once a week, never drink alone, and consume no more than three drinks at a time.

Ask yourself the following questions:

- How many nights a week do I drink?
- Do I have more than two drinks a night (if you are a woman), or more than three (if you are a man)?
- Do I feel an effect from the alcohol?
- How do I feel on the days I drink and a few days after?
- How much am I focusing on my "drinking days"?

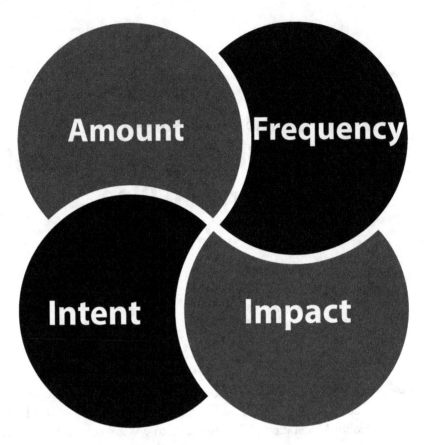

Image 11.1 Quick Check

Paying attention to how you feel on a drinking day is helpful. If that is the one day you look forward to all week, you still have work to do. Explore what is so bad about your day-to-day life that you crave this outlet. See what other activities you can look forward to doing.

You may be tempted to make regular exceptions to your Alcohol Moderation Plan. Holidays, graduations, weddings, birthdays, free tickets to a game, and sports playoffs will come up. However, there is no reason you cannot enjoy these events without alcohol. Find something other than drinking to focus attention on: the people, the game, the food, or the celebratory aspect of the event.

What amount am I drinking now?

_____

_____

_____

Frequency

Checking the frequency of alcohol use is similar to monitoring the amount. It should fall within the moderation guidelines. Watch out for how often you are drinking and if you are seeking out increasing situations where alcohol will be present. What it is like when you do not drink? You may surprise yourself when you realize you do not miss drinking as much as you thought and enjoy the benefits of an alcohol-free event.

What is the frequency of my moderate drinking?

_____

_____

_____

Intent

Be aware of *why* you are drinking. If you are looking to change your mood or to cope with emotions, you need to develop alternative ways to manage. Identify someone who has their life together. It can be someone you know or even a television, movie, or book character. Observe what they do and how they do it. Then emulate what they do.

If you are feeling an effect from the alcohol you consume, reevaluate the amount you are taking in. Identify why you place such a high priority on drinking. Pay attention to how you feel when you drink. If this is the only time you are happy or feel normal, you have more work to do. I typically recommend returning to a period of abstinence to get distance from alcohol and establish a new baseline.

Notice how you feel on nondrinking nights. If you feel bored, miserable, or left out, you may be focusing only on what you are losing, not on what you are gaining. Identify other ways to relax, socialize, and have fun. This takes time, especially if past alcohol consumption has damaged some of the neurotransmitters in your brain that allows you to feel pleasure and happiness. It can take several months to repair the effects that alcohol has had on your body.

Also, if you are struggling on nondrinking nights, you may have not allowed enough time to adjust to the new lifestyle. Any change takes time to feel normal. It may take several months, but most people report feeling significantly better after six months, and certainly by a year.

What is the intent of my moderate drinking?

_____

_____

_____

Impact

My goal is not to have you relive all the bad times related to problematic drinking patterns, but to be honest about whether they are still occurring once you return to alcohol use. Explore what happens now when you drink. If you are not getting the "stink eye" from your family members, no one is complaining, and you are happy, you may have developed a very good plan. I encourage you to take a risk and ask loved ones for their observations on your current drinking. You may be pleasantly surprised to hear what they have to say about you now. Be realistic with whose opinions you consider. Asking your old drinking buddies how you are doing with your new drinking pattern will yield very different responses from those of the people you live with and may have hurt.

What is the impact of my moderate drinking?

_____

_____

_____

As noted earlier, a lapse or a relapse is an opportunity to learn what was not working. Having a lapse in problematic drinking is not always a bad thing. It is an opportunity to address areas that you may not have considered or been realistic about when you first developed the plan. For alcohol moderators, returning to drinking is not a relapse. The relapse is when consequences begin to occur. Sometimes lapses help everyone to take the situation more seriously. It is easy to fall back into old patterns.

HALT

HALT is an acronym that stands for: Hungry, Angry, Lonely, Tired. HALT translates to "stop" in German. Stop, take a moment to reflect, and take action if you need to address any of these areas. If any of them are out of balance, you are more likely to make poor choices.

Hungry: Think about how poorly you feel when you are hungry. When my blood sugar gets low, I get a headache, am irritable, and can't concentrate. If you are physically hungry, make sure you refuel with some healthy food. If you know you are going to have a long workday, car ride, or carpool, plan ahead for meals and healthy snacks like fruits, nuts, cheese, yogurt, or protein bars. Don't forget to stay hydrated.

Hungry can also refer to how we feel emotionally. If you are bored with your routine, do something to mix it up. Spend time with someone you have not seen in a while, take a road trip, or try an activity you have never done before.

When are you hungry? What can you do about it?

_____

_____

_____

Angry: When we are angry or experiencing negative emotions, we often do not think rationally. If you are angry, take some time to calm down, talk with a friend, and then address the problem. If it is a chronic issue, break it down into manageable tasks. Just taking even one step forward can make you feel less hopeless and helpless about a situation. If you are emotional, I also recommend waiting at least two hours and talking to another person before you touch technology. This means no texting, tweeting, e-mailing, or posting. You don't want to put something out in cyberspace that you will regret later.

When are you angry? What can you do to address it?

_____

_____

_____

Lonely: We all experience loneliness at times in our lives. Though we may be surrounded by people, we often are not interacting with them. Despite all of our modern technology, many of us are plugged in but not connected. Think about the number of times you have made a problem much worse in your head, turning the situation into a catastrophe. However, once you talked it out, you gained a much more positive perspective. Reach out every day and connect face-to-face with other people. Isolation can be a breeding ground for depression and unhealthy choices.

When do you experience loneliness? What steps can you take to manage it?

_____

_____

_____

Tired: When we are physically and emotionally tired, we tend to engage in more negative thinking patterns and interactions. Make sure that you get enough sleep at night. Practice good sleep hygiene. It's a funny phrase, as if people are dirty sleepers, but it refers to developing habits that make restful sleep more conducive. This includes getting up and going to bed around the same time each day, reducing distractions that interrupt sleep (pets, television, or phone), monitoring caffeine and sugar intake, managing stressors, and limiting exposure to bright lights, which interrupts the biological process that allows melatonin levels to rise and help us drift off to sleep.

When do you get tired? What can you do to deal with it?

_____

_____

_____

DID YOU KNOW? Saliva regenerates every 10 to 15 minutes. Law enforcement and treatment providers know this. The excuses of "I just used mouthwash" or "I took some cough syrup" are not accurate explanations for testing positive for alcohol on a breath test. You would have to actually drink the mouthwash or consume a large quantity of cold medicine to register positive. Initially, a Breathalyzer would read very high if you had just used rinsed your mouth or swallowed it, but then 15 minutes later, nothing readable would remain.[88]

Tangible Reminders

As I described in Chapter 9, tangible reminders are things that we can see, feel, touch, and hold that remind us of the changes we are trying to make in our lives regarding alcohol. Keep reminders in convenient areas such as on the bathroom mirror, on your physical person, in the car, on the phone, and in the workspace. Have both positive and negative reminders to help you stay focused and accountable to your Alcohol Moderation Plan.

What tangible reminders can you use?

_____

_____

_____

Daily Checks

Pick a specific time each day to reflect on your mood, goals, and achievements. Notice that I did not say to look at where you did not do well. Most of us do this to ourselves anyway, agonizing over what we said or did or didn't do. Classic behavioral reinforcement notes that the behaviors we pay attention to are the ones that get reinforced. Think about that. If all we focus on is what we did wrong, we will keep doing it. But if we look at our successes, we can figure out how to build upon them and will be much happier as a result.

Pick a specific time each day to reflect. Some people choose times such as when they are on their way home from work, when they exercise, or when they shower. These are things you may not do every day. Reflect when you brush your teeth or right before bed. A daily check takes just a few moments. If you are experiencing a negative emotion, consider proactive ways of dealing with it. Check if your HALT is in balance or how you are doing on your Quick Check. If areas need attention, identify a plan to address them.

Another type of daily check is scaling. It's not how much you weigh, but how you feel. On a scale of 1 to 10, with 10 being the best day ever and 1 being the worst, where are you today? If you are anywhere from a 7 to a 10, identify the factors that helped create this feeling and repeat them if they are healthy behaviors. If you are below a 4, it might be important to reach out to a friend or a professional. It is completely normal to have a bad day occasionally, sometimes for no apparent reason. But if the bad days continue for more than a week, try to identify the stressor and what can be done to correct it. If the bad days last for more than two weeks or start affecting activities of daily living, it may be time to seek therapy.

Some people like to keep a journal or a mood tracker. There are also many great apps on smartphones that can help you with this. Don't compare to anyone but yourself. Ask, "Am I feeling better or worse today than I did yesterday?" When you track your numbers, thoughts, and feelings, you may notice trends and patterns. That way you can identify the triggers that lead to negative moods and increase the actions that prompt the healthy ones.

What daily check will you use?

_____

_____

_____

Weekly Checks

Performing weekly checks is important at the beginning of abstinence as well as once you start practicing moderation. Again, I recommend selecting a specific day and time to review. In the first few months, this may be a therapist, support group, or online posting. Eventually, you may transition to a friend, partner, or other support people. By having a specific day, person, and time scheduled, you are more likely to review your successes and struggles. Additionally, if you do not connect, your support person should come looking, increasing accountability.

What weekly check can you use?

_____

_____

_____

Monthly Checks

I suggest picking a specific day each month for a planned meeting or activity such as meeting with your counselor, attending a support group, driving by the site where the DUI occurred, or reviewing your Alcohol Moderation Plan with your support person. If you say you will do it once a month, you may not follow through. If you chose a date that is significant to you, like the anniversary of your lifestyle change or the date you implemented your plan, you are more likely to stick to it.

What monthly check will you practice?

_____

_____

_____

Preparing to Drink Again

No one teaches you how to do this or what to expect. We have been so programmed that abstinence is the only way drinkers experiencing problems can be healthy and is the way most programs determine success. Remember that people tend to have better outcomes in alcohol moderation when they go through a period of abstinence.

Hillary's experience gives a good idea of what might happen when you return to drinking:

Hillary was in her late 20s. After a period of significant emotional and relationship turmoil resulting from her cocaine, marijuana, and alcohol use, she entered therapy and went through a period of complete abstinence. Hillary understood the role drugs played in her life and worked hard to find new ways to have fun, utilize the coping skills she had learned, and develop relationships with people who were advancing in their adult lives.

After she had been substance-free for over six months, we used therapy sessions to prepare her to try alcohol moderation. She consistently reported that cocaine was the chemical she'd had the most problems with and planned never to use it or marijuana again. She chose a specific drink that she actually enjoyed the taste of, met with a healthy friend who supported her drinking goals, and chose an environment where she had never had a bad drinking or emotional episode.

Hillary was not prepared for the emotions stirred up by losing her clean date (the day after last substance use). She no longer felt the special feeling that sobriety had brought to her life. She had been keeping track of the days that marked the end of her unhealthy life and the start of a new one.

Hillary was also not prepared for the feelings of guilt that surfaced. During the time when she was not using any substances, she had felt as if she was making up for all the poor decisions and actions that had hurt her friends and family. Once she had the first drink, however, she felt as though she had lost their forgiveness.

Through unexpected tears, Hillary realized she had more work to do. She decided to remain alcohol-free for a few more months while she worked on her feelings about her past, repaired her relationships, and identified who she would like to be in the future.

In this scenario, Hillary was going through a process that I call integration. Integration is accepting who you were and what you did when you were drinking in an unhealthy way. It means not only seeking forgiveness from those you hurt but also forgiving yourself.

People in early recovery tend to spend a lot of time reliving the past, which was often destructive, unhealthy, and emotionally painful. While it is important to acknowledge the mistakes of the past, we cannot live there if we are going to stay healthy in the long run. The same is true for the present. It is important to stay connected and mindful of what is happening in the moment, but we also need to prepare for a healthier, happier future. Only once we integrate our past self into who we are in the present do we really begin to move forward emotionally. When I see people feeling comfortable with who they are right now and getting excited about something in the future, I know they have completed the integration process.

Chapter Twelve
Alcohol Moderation Resources

This final chapter outlines moderation-friendly programs and resources that are available throughout the world. Mutual support programs and dry month campaigns are included.

Mutual Support Groups for Alcohol Moderation

There are increasing types of mutual support groups worldwide that can assist you. Below are the more established programs and mutual support groups that support alcohol moderation:

Moderation Management
www.moderation.org

Moderation Management (MM) is a nonprofit dedicated to reducing the harm caused by the abuse of alcohol. They focus on self-management, balance, moderation, and personal responsibility. The program encourages individuals to accept responsibility for maintaining their own recovery path. MM promotes early recognition of risky drinking so that moderate drinking is more likely to be achieved.

   MM offers a mutual-help environment that encourages people who are concerned about their drinking to take action before drinking problems become severe. They offer a nine-step professionally reviewed program that includes information about alcohol, moderate drinking guidelines, monitoring exercises, goal setting tools, and self-management strategies. In addition, MM provides listings of moderation-friendly therapists, online forums, chat groups, and face-to-face meetings. They also run the Dryuary™ Challenge.

Hello Sunday Morning
www.hellosundaymorning.org

Hello Sunday Morning (HSM) is an online support community with health campaigns and behavior change programs designed to help people who want to change their relationship to alcohol in a confidential environment. It was started in 2009 by Australian Chris Raine, a nightclub promoter who began blogging about taking a year off from drinking. He wrote about how he would wake up each Sunday morning hangover-free, singing "Hello Sunday morning!" HSM's mission is to change the world's relationship with alcohol. The relationship can be abstaining, taking a break, or understanding how to have a healthy relationship with alcohol.

HAMS Harm Reduction Network
www.hamsnetwork.org

The HAMS Harm Reduction Network (HAMS) provides information and support for people who wish to reduce the harm in their lives caused by the use of alcohol or drugs. HAMS stands for harm reduction, alcohol abstinence, and moderation support. They support the goals of safer drinking, reduced drinking, or quitting. Participants choose the goal and may switch it at any time. Hamsnetwork.org lists treatment providers who support safer alcohol use and also offers online forums, chat groups, written materials, podcasts, and live meetings. They neither encourage nor condemn alcohol use or alcohol intoxication, but recognize recreational use as a reality and seek to reduce harms associated with it. HAMS believes in the autonomy of the individual and supports each individual's choice of a goal regarding their alcohol use.

SMART Recovery
www.smartrecovery.org

SMART Recovery is a self-empowering addiction-recovery support group. SMART stands for self-management and recovery training. They offer meetings around the world, including the United States, Canada, Denmark, Australia, Ireland, and the United Kingdom. Participants learn to use tools based on the latest scientific research and attend self-help groups. SMART offers a four-point program with tools and techniques for each. This includes building and maintaining motivation; coping with urges; managing thoughts, feelings, and behaviors; and living a balanced life. SMART is typically for those wanting to achieve abstinence, but people wanting to try moderation are still invited to participate.

Alcohol Moderation Programs

CheckUp & Choices

Reid Hester, PhD, cofounded CheckUp & Choices with Canton Burtwell. Their goal was to help individuals and organizations realize their potential by helping them reduce alcohol and drug problems. They developed the web-based program to be used on any internet device. The program is listed as an evidence-based program by the Substance Abuse and Mental Health Services Administration.

The first phase, called CheckUps, includes a confidential alcohol self-assessment where participants receive feedback on their responses. The second phase, Choices, is a 3- to 12-month program and can be used for those who wish to abstain from alcohol as well as those who want to moderate their use. Individuals receive motivational exercises, drink, mood and urge trackers, guided emails, and change plans.

The Sinclair Method

The Sinclair Method (TSM) was developed by the late Dr. David Sinclair. It involves taking Naltrexone (also known as Nalmefene in other countries) one hour prior to drinking alcohol to create "pharmacological extinction." It is the epitome of alcohol moderation, as the program does not require people to be alcohol-free. Its goal is to reduce episodes of heavy drinking.

Sinclair began studying behavioral reinforcement in the 1960s. He theorized that people develop problems with drinking though learned behavior. Each time a person consumes alcohol, the brain releases endorphins, which strengthen synapses in the brain. The more the synapses grow, the more a person thinks about and craves alcohol. Sinclair speculated that an opiate agonist (blocking) medication would weaken the synapses, thus extinguishing the craving by blocking the reinforcing effects of alcohol in the brain. Reports show that it has a 78% effectiveness for reducing the amount consumed to safer levels while a quarter of users achieve complete abstinence.

DID YOU KNOW? Heavy alcohol users may consume more calories in their drinks than in their food, causing weight gain and nutritional deficiencies. Light beers have about 100 calories per serving, the average glass of wine has about 120, and an ounce of liquor is around 100. Add in mixers and the calorie and sugar count goes up. For example, A 12-ounce margarita can have 680 calories. If someone drinks three, they have reached their recommended daily caloric intake.[89]

Dry Month Campaigns

There are growing numbers of dry month campaigns, with names like Dryuary, Dry Feb, and October. They ask participations to commit to a month of being alcohol-free. Some raise money for public health concerns like cancer, while others focus on health benefits and offer education, motivation, and support. Participating in one of them may help you archive a period of abstinence and feel like you are doing something good for someone else.

Congratulations!

Congratulations on making it to the end of this workbook! My hope is that you now have the information, tools, and resources to have a healthier relationship with alcohol. This may mean changing the amount, frequency, and situations in which you drink. You may even have decided to quit. Ultimately, you decide what alcohol moderation looks like for you. I wish you a happy, healthy, balanced life!

References

1. Egelko, B. (2007, September 8). Appeals court say requirement to attend AA unconstitutional. *San Francisco Chronicle*.
2. Substance Abuse and Mental Health Services Administration. (2012, February). *What's recovery? SAMHSA's working definition*. Publication ID: PEP12-RECDEF.
3. U.S. Department of Health and Human Services (HHS), Office of the Surgeon General. (2016, November). *Facing addiction in America: The surgeon general's report on alcohol, drugs, and health*. Washington, DC: HHS.
4. Harm Reduction Coalition. (2011). Edith Springer: Goddess of harm reduction. Interview. Retrieved from http://harmreduction.org/publication-type/podcast/forty-two/
5. Springer, E. (1991). Effective AIDS prevention with active drug users: The harm reduction model. In M. Shernoff (Ed.), *Counseling chemically dependent people with HIV illness* (pp. 141–158). New York: Harrington Park Press.
6. Tatarsky, A. & Marlatt, A. (2010). State of the art in harm reduction psychotherapy: An emerging treatment for substance misuse. *Journal of Clinical Psychology: In Session* 66(2): 117–122. doi: 10.1002/jclp.20672
7. Denning, P. & Little, J. (2017). *Over the influence: The harm reduction guide to controlling your drug and alcohol use* (2nd ed.). New York: The Guilford Press.
8. Mann, K., Aubin, H.-J. & Witikiewitz, K. (2017, September 22). Reduced drinking in alcohol dependence treatment, what is the evidence? *European Addiction Research* 23: 219–230. doi: 10.1159/000481348
9. Kodjak, A. (2016, June 16). Inventors see big opportunities in opioid addiction treatment. *NPR*. Retrieved from www.npr.org/sections/health-shots/2016/06/10/480663056/investors-see-big-opportunities-in-opioid-addiction-treatment
10. Turner, C. (2020). *The clinician's guide to alcohol moderation: Alternative methods and management techniques*. New York, NY: Routledge.
11. Miller, W.R. (2019, July 7). Personal communication.
12. Miller, W.R. & Munoz, R.F. (2013). *Controlling your drinking, 2nd ed: Tools to make moderation work for you*. New York: The Guilford Press.
13. U.S. Department of Health and Human Services and U.S. Department of Agriculture. (2015). *2015–2020 Dietary Guidelines for Americans* (External 8th ed.). Washington, DC.
14. American Heart Association. (2014, August 15). Alcohol and heart health. Retrieved from www.heart.org/en/healthy-living/healthy-eating/eat-smart/nutrition-basics/alcohol-and-heart-health
15. National Institute of Alcohol Abuse and Alcoholism. (2016, May). *Rethinking drinking: Alcohol and your health*. Retrieved from www.rethinkingdrinking.niaaa.nih.gov/

16. Alcohol in Moderation. (2018, September). Sensible drinking guidelines. Retrieved from www.drinkingandyou.com/site/pdf/Sensibledrinking.pdf

17. Peele, S. (2015, June 8). Studies show that drinking problems are increasing: Here's why. *The Fix*. Retrieved from www.thefix.com/content/we-have-more-drinking-problems-why/

18. Rotgers, F., Kern, M.F. & Hoeltzel, R. (2002). *Responsible drinking: A moderation management approach for problem drinkers*. Oakland, CA: New Harbinger Publications.

19. United States Census Bureau. (2019, March 11). Retrieved from www.census.gov

20. Substance Abuse and Mental Health Services Administration. (2018). *Key substance use and mental health indicators in the United States: Results from the 2017 National Survey on Drug Use and Health* (HHS Publication No. SMA 18-5068, NSDUH Series H-53). Rockville, MD: Center for Behavioral Health Statistics and Quality, Substance Abuse and Mental Health Services Administration. Retrieved from www.samhsa.gov/data/

21. World Health Organization. (2014). Global status report on alcohol and health: 2014 ed. Retrieved from www.who.int/substance_abuse/publications/global_alcohol_report/msb_gsr_2014_1.pdf

22. Moderation Management. (2019, March 27). Retrieved from www.moderation.org/about_mm/whatismm.html

23. Esser, M.B., Hedden, S.L., Kanny, D., Brewer, R.D., Gfroerer, J.C. & Naimi, J.C. (2014). Prevalence of alcohol dependence among US adult drinkers, 2009–2001. *Preventing Chronic Disease* 11: 140329. http://dx.doi.org/10.5888/pcd11.140329

24. Turner, C. (2020). *The clinician's guide to alcohol moderation: Alternative methods and management techniques*. New York, NY: Routledge.

25. American Psychiatric Association. (2013). *Diagnostic and statistical manual of mental disorders* (5th ed.). Washington, DC: American Psychiatric Association.

26. Keller, M. & Valliant, G.E. (2019, April 24). Alcoholism. *Encyclopedia Britannica*. Retrieved from www.britannica.com/science/alcoholism.

27. American Psychiatric Association. (2013). *Diagnostic and statistical manual of mental disorders* (5th ed.). Washington, DC: American Psychiatric Association.

28. Turner, C. (2020). *The clinician's guide to alcohol moderation: Alternative methods and management techniques*. New York, NY: Routledge.

29. Griswold, M.G., Fullman, N., Hawley, C., Arian, N., Zimsen, S., Tymeson, H.D., Venkateswaran, V., Tapp, A.D., Forouzanfar, M., Salama, J.S., Abate, K., Abate, D., Abay, S., Abbafati, C., Suliankatchi, R., Zegeye, A., Aboyans, V., Abrar, M.M. & Acharya, P. (2018). Alcohol use and burden for 195 countries and territories, 1990–2016: A systematic analysis for the Global Burden of Disease Study 2016. *Lancet* 392: 1015–1035.

30. Mayo Clinic. (2019, March 11). Red wine and resveratrol: Good for your heart? Retrieved from www.mayoclinic.org/diseases-conditions/heart-disease/in-depth/red-wine/art-20048281

31. Newman, T. (2017, December 22). All about the central nervous system. *Medical News Today*.

32. Banerjee, N. (2014). Neurotransmitters in alcoholism: A review of neurobiological and genetic studies. *Indian Journal of Human Genetics* 20(1): 20–31. doi: 10.4103/0971-6866.132750

33. Piano, M.R. (2017). Alcohol's effects on the cardiovascular system. *Alcohol Research* 38(2): 219–241.

34. Nordqvist, C. (2018, February 6). What's to know about liver disease? *Medical News Today*. Retrieved from www.medicalnewstoday.com/articles/215638.php

35. Chowdhury, P. & Gupta, P. (2006). Pathology of alcoholic pancreatitis: An overview. *World Journal of Gastroenterology* 12(46): 7421–7427. doi: 10.3748/wjg.v12.i46.7421

36. Sarkar, D., Jung, M.K. & Wang, H.J. (2015). Alcohol and the immune system. *Alcohol Research: Current Reviews* 37(2): 153–155.

37. May, P.A. & Gossage, J.P. (2011). Fetal alcohol spectrum disorders. *Alcohol Research and Health* 34(1): 16–23.

38. National Highway Traffic Safety Administration. (2018). *Traffic safety Facts 2016 data: Alcohol-impaired driving*. Washington, DC: U.S. Department of Transportation. Retrieved from https://crashstats.nhtsa.dot.gov/Api/Public/ViewPublication/812450External

39. Zhao, X., Zhang, X. & Rong, J. (2014). Study of the effects of alcohol on drivers and driving performance on straight road. *Mathematical Problems in Engineering*. Article ID 607652. https://doi.org/10.1155/2014/607652

40. Wells, S., Graham, K. & West, P. (2000, July). Alcohol-related aggression in the general population. *Journal of Studies on Alcohol* 61(4): 626–632.

41. National Sleep Foundation. (2019, May 5). How alcohol affects the quality-and quantity of sleep. Retrieved from www.sleepfoundation.org/articles/how-alcohol-affects-quality-and-quantity-sleep

42. National Health Service. (2018, May 30). Sleep and tiredness: Why lack of sleep is bad for your health. Retrieved from www.nhs.uk/live-well/sleep-and-tiredness/why-lack-of-sleep-is-bad-for-your-health/

43. Bush, B. & Hudson, T. (2010). The role of cortisol in sleep. *Natural Medicine Journal* 2(6).

44. Usman, M. (2019, February 2). How does alcohol consumption affect your weight and shape? Retrieved from www.weightlossresources.co.uk/body_weight/alcohol-effect.htm

45. Winter, C. (2017, January 11). Why does alcohol make you hungry? Biological link between drinking and binge eating discovered. *ABC.net.AUNews.* Retrieved from www.abc.net.au/news/2017-01-11/why-does-alcohol-make-you-hungry/8176220

46. Cains, S. *et al.* (2017). Agrp neuron activity is required for alcohol-induced overeating. *Nature Communication* 8: 14014. doi: 10.1038/ncomms14014

47. Prochaska, J.O., DiClemente, C.C. & Norcross, J.C. (1992). In search of how people change: Applications to the addictive behaviors. *American Psychologist* 47: 1102–1114. PMID: 1329589.

48. Prochaska, J.O., Norcross, J.C. & DiClemente, C.C. (1994). *Changing for good.* New York: Morrow. ISBN: 0-380-72572-X.

49. Selk, J. (2013, April 15). Habit formation: The 21-day myth. *Forbes.com.* Retrieved from www.forbes.com/sites/jasonselk/2013/04/15/habit-formation-the-21-day-myth/#48ee9dcddebc

50. Witte, K. & Allen, M. (2000). A meta-analysis of fear appeals: Implications for effective public health programs. *Health Education and Behavior* 27(5): 591–615.

51. Sanchez-Craig, M. (2013). *Saying when: How to quit drinking or cut down.* Toronto, Canada: Center for Addiction and Mental Health.

52. Kadam, M., Sinha, A., Nimkar, S., Matcheswalla, Y. & De Sousa, A. (2017). A comparative study of factors associated with relapse in alcohol dependence and opioid dependence. *Indian Journal of Psychological Medicine* 39(5): 627–633. doi: 10.4103/IJPSYM.IJPSYM_356_17

53. National Institute on Alcohol Abuse and Alcoholism. (1998, July). *Alcohol alert no. 41.* Bethesda, MD.

54. Witikiewitz, K., Bowen, S., Harropt, E.N., Douglas, H., Enkema, M. & Sedgwick. (2014). Mindfulness-based treatment to prevent addictive behavior relapse: Theoretical models and hypothesized mechanisms of change. *Substance Use and Misuse* 49(5): 513–524. doi: 10.3109/10826084.2014.891845

55. Zakhari, S. (2019, March 9). Overview: How is alcohol metabolized by the body? *National Institutes on Alcohol Abuse and Alcoholism.* Retrieved from https://pubs.niaaa.nih.gov/publications/arh294/245-255.htm

56. Ostafin, B.D. & Marlatt, G.A. (2008). Surfing the urge: Experiential acceptance moderates the relation between automatic alcohol motivation and hazardous drinking. *Journal of Social and Clinical Psychology* 27(4): 404–418. https://doi.org/10.1521/jscp.2008.27.4.404

57. Griffin, K. (2010). Interview with G. Alan Marlatt: Surfing the Urge. *Inquiring Mind.* 26(2).

58. National Institute on Alcohol Abuse and Alcoholism. (2018, October). Understanding the dangers of alcohol overdose. Retrieved from https://pubs.niaaa.nih.gov/publications/AlcoholOverdoseFactsheet/Overdosefact.htm

59. Khooury, L., Tang, Y.L., Bradley, B., Cubells, J.F. & Ressler, K.J. (2010, December). Substance use, childhood traumatic experience, and post traumatic stress disorder in an urban civilian population. *Depression and Anxiety* 27(12): 1077–1086.

60. National Child Traumatic Stress Network. (2008). *Understanding links between adolescent trauma and substance abuse: A toolkit for providers* (2nd ed.). Retrieved from www.nctsn.org/resources/understanding-links-between-adolescent-trauma-and-substance-abuse-toolkit-providers-2nd

61. Volpicelli, J., Balaraman, G., Hahn, J., Wallace, H. & Bux, D. (1999). The role of uncontrollable trauma in the development of PTSD and alcohol addiction. *Alcohol Research and Health* 23(4): 256–262.

62. Bombardier, C.H. & Turner, A. (2009). Alcohol and traumatic disability. In R. Frank & T. Elliott (Eds.), *The handbook of rehabilitation psychology* (2nd ed., pp. 241–258). Washington, DC: American Psychological Association Press.

63. American Academy of Experts in Traumatic Stress website. (2016, December 14). Effects of parental substance abuse on children and families. Retrieved from www.aaets.org/article230.htm

64. Center for Behavioral Health Statistics and Quality. (2015). *Behavioral health trends in the United States: Results from the 2014 National Survey on Drug Use and Health* (HHS Publication No. SMA 15-4927, NSDUH Series H-50). Retrieved from www.samhsa.gov/data/

65. National Alliance on Mental Illness. (2019, May 14). Retrieved from www.nami.org/Find-Support/Living-with-a-Mental-Health-Condition/Taking-Care-of-Your-Body/Drugs-Alcohol-Smoking

66. Edenberg, H.J. (2003, June). *The collaborative study on the genetics of alcoholism: An update*. Bethesda, MD: National Institute on Alcohol Abuse and Alcoholism.

67. Hall, C.W. & Webster, R.E. (2007). Risk factors among adult children of alcoholics. *International Journal of Behavioral Consultation and Therapy* 3(4): 494–511. http://dx.doi.org/10

68. Trevisan, L.A., Boutrous, N., Petrakis, I.L. & Krystal, J.H. (1998). Complications of alcohol withdrawal: Pathophysiological insights. *Alcohol Health & Research World* 22(1): 61–66.

69. Davis, C.P. & Shiel, W.C., Jr. (2019, March 7). Liver blood tests (normal, low, and high ranges & results). *MedicineNet*. Retrieved from www.medicinenet.com/liver_blood_tests/article.htm#what_are_the_basic_functions_of_the_liver

70. Newman, T. (2018, March 2). What does the liver do? *Medical News Today*. Retrieved from www.medical newstoday.com/articles/305075.php

71. Smolen, J. (2018, October 6). Binge drinking and blackouts: The sobering truth about lost learning in students. *Neurocise News*.

72. White, A.M. (2003). What happened? Alcohol, memory, blackouts, and the brain. *Alcohol Research and Health* 27(2): 186–196.

73. Sweeney, D.F. (2011). Take blackouts seriously. *Addiction Professional* 9(4): 54–57.

74. Grant, B.F. & Dawson, D.A. (1997). Age of onset of alcohol use and its association with DSM-IV alcohol use and dependence: Results from the National Longitudinal Alcohol Epidemiological Survey. *Journal of Substance Abuse* 9: 103–110.

75. Clapp, P.C., Bhave, S.V. & Hoffman, P.L. (2009). How adaptation of the brain to alcohol leads to dependence: A pharmacological perspective. *National Institute of Alcohol Abuse and Alcoholism*. Retrieved from https://pubs.niaaa.nih.gov/publications/arh314/310-339.htm

76. National Institute on Drug Abuse, National Institutes of Health & U.S. Department of Health and Human Services. (2003). *Preventing drug use among children and adolescents* (In brief). Rockville, MD.

77. Johnston, L.D., O'Malley, P.M., Bachman, J.G. & Schulenberg, J.E. (2007). *Monitoring the future: National results on adolescent drug use: Overview of key findings, 2006*. Bethesda, MD: National Institute on Drug Abuse.

78. Sanchez-Craig, M., Annis, H.M., Bronet, A.R. & MacDonald, K.R. (1984). Random assignment to abstinence and controlled drinking: Evaluation of a cognitive-behavioral program for problem drinkers. *Journal of Consulting and Clinical Psychology* 52(3): 390–403. http://dx.doi.org/10.1037/0022-006X.52.3.390

79. National Highway Traffic Safety Administration. (2016). *The abc of bac: A guide to understanding blood alcohol concentration and impairment*. Washington, DC: US Department of Transportation.

80. Cornett, D. (2005). *7 weeks to safe social drinking: How to effectively moderate your alcohol intake*. Santa Rosa, CA: People Friendly Books.

81. Cederbaum, A.I. (2012). Alcohol metabolism. *Clinics in Liver Disease* 16(4): 667–685. doi: 10.1016/j.cld.2012.08.002

82. Drinkaware. (2019, June 1). Alcohol and mental health. Retrieved from www.drinkaware.co.uk/alcohol-facts/health-effects-of-alcohol/mental-health/alcohol-and-mental-health/

83. Dean, N. (2018). The importance of novelty. *Brain World*. Retrieved from https://brainworldmagazine.com/the-importance-of-novelty/

84. Aron, A., Norman, C., Aron, E., McKenna, C. & Heyman, R. (2000). Couples' shared participation in novel and arousing activities and experienced relationship quality. *Social Psychology* 78(2): 273–284. doi: 10.1037//0022-3514.78.2.273

85. Cheng, Y.Y.B. & Staduinger, U.M. (2018). Novelty processing at work and cognitive aging: Evidence from the health and retirement study and midus. *Innovation in Aging* 2(1). https://doi.org/10.1093/geroni/igy023.1585

86. Rotgers, F., Kern, M.F. & Hoeltzel, R. (2002). *Responsible drinking: A moderation management approach for problem drinkers*. Oakland, CA: New Harbinger Publications.

87. Shukla, L., Sharma, P., Ganesha, S., Ghadigaonkar, D., Thomas, E., Kandas, A., Murthy, P. & Benegal, V. (2017). Value of ethyl glucuronide and ethyl sulfate in serum as biomarkers of alcohol consumption. *Indian Journal of Psychological Medicine* 39(4): 481–487.

88. Tiwari, M. (2011). Science behind human saliva. *Journal of Natural Science, Biology and Medicine* 2(1): 53–58. doi: 10.4103/0976-9668.82322

89. National Institute on Alcohol Abuse and Alcoholism. (2019, March 11). Alcohol calorie calculator. Retrieved from www.rethinkingdrinking.niaaa.nih.gov/Tools/Calculators/Calorie-Calculator.aspx

Index

Page numbers in italic type indicate figures.

Printed in the United States
by Baker & Taylor Publisher Services